TRANSKEI'S HALF LOAF

TRANSKEI'S HALF LOAF

RACE SEPARATISM IN SOUTH AFRICA

NEWELL M. STULTZ

NEW HAVEN AND LONDON
YALE UNIVERSITY PRESS
1979

DESIGNED BY THOS. WHITRIDGE
AND SET IN IBM BASKERVILLE TYPE.
PRINTED IN THE UNITED STATES OF AMERICA BY
HALLIDAY LITHOGRAPH, WEST HANOVER, MASS.

PUBLISHED IN GREAT BRITAIN, EUROPE, AFRICA,
AND ASIA (EXCEPT JAPAN) BY YALE UNIVERSITY
PRESS, LTD., LONDON. DISTRIBUTED IN AUSTRALIA
AND NEW ZEALAND BY BOOK & FILM SERVICES,
ARTARMON, N.S.W., AUSTRALIA; AND IN JAPAN BY
HARPER & ROW, PUBLISHERS, TOKYO OFFICE.

LIBRARY OF CONGRESS CATALOGING IN PUBLICATION DATA
Stultz, Newell Maynard.
    Transkei's half loaf.

    Bibliography: p.
    Includes index.
    1. Transkei—Politics and government.
2. South Africa—Politics and government—
1961–   3. South Africa—Race relations.
I. Title.
DT846.T7S78   320.9'68'7   78-65481
ISBN 0-300-02333-2

FOR MY PARENTS

CONTENTS

PREFACE

Most of the research on which this book is based was undertaken in Transkei and South Africa (then still legally joined) over a period of three months during the second half of 1976. The climax of this visit, and also its conclusion, was the opportunity to be present together with 25,000 others for the Transkei independence celebrations at Umtata on the evening of October 25. Thirteen years earlier (November–December 1963) I had been in Transkei for political events which at that time were also unprecedented—the first Transkei general election and the election and installation of the first Transkei cabinet. On the basis of this experience I later wrote, with Gwendolen M. Carter and Thomas Karis, a book entitled *South Africa's Transkei: The Politics of Domestic Colonialism* (Evanston: Northwestern University Press, 1967). This was contemporary history. We were pleased with its acceptance, but a decade later it was obviously dated. I returned to Transkei in 1976 to refresh my knowledge of the region.

In 1963 serious scholarship on Transkei was limited, most of it undertaken at nearby Rhodes University in the Department of Anthropology by Philip Mayer and David Hammond-Tooke. When *South Africa's Transkei* appeared in 1967, it had few competitors in the fields of history or political science. In retrospect it appears that we three Americans

made a contribution to the fund of empirical information
South Africans of all races have about themselves. Ten years
later, at the level of empiricism, the scholar from overseas
who is interested in Transkei has greater difficulty being
original. For while there are still too few Transkeians interested or prepared to study their own country, the number of
white South Africans with this interest has grown appreciably.
Among them are Nancy C. J. Charton, Gillian P. Hart, W. J.
Breytenbach, Johann Maree, F. van Zyl Slabbert, Robert
Schrire, and D. A. Kotze, in addition to Philip Mayer and
David Hammond-Tooke, whose work on Transkei continues.

In terms of my own efforts, the greatest challenge came
not from a professional scholar, but from a working journalist, Patrick Laurence, a reporter on the *Rand Daily Mail* in
Johannesburg. Only days before Transkei independence on
October 25, Ravan Press in Johannesburg published a book
by Laurence entitled *The Transkei: South Africa's Politics
of Partition*. As several newspaper reviewers immediately perceived, the Laurence book, though not long, is an important
political history of Transkei up to the eve of its independence. Rich in factual information, well documented and
intelligent, it is impressively grounded in the relevant academic literature. (In fact, Laurence holds a master's degree in
history from the University of Natal.) With the appearance of
this book, it seems apparent that further empirical work on
Transkei politics at the level of macro-studies should focus on
the period *after* independence. For regarding the facts of the
situation, Laurence has probably told his readers as much
about Transkei politics up to October 1976 as they can reasonably be expected to want to know.

Yet sitting among the crowd at Independence Stadium in
Umtata on the evening of October 25, I realized that none of
the academic and other serious writers on Transkei was very
helpful (at the level of ideas rather than of facts) in suggesting a meaning for the event we were observing. In the opening paragraphs of his book Laurence compares the decision
of Transkei to choose independence in 1976 with the suicidal
decision of the AmaXhosa 120 years before to slaughter their
cattle and consume their grain, as the prophetess Nongquase

had directed, in order to drive away the white man. But in the clearest deficiency of his work, Laurence does not return to this or indeed come to any other conclusion at the end of his book. I mean no disrespect in observing that he chooses to be a reporter rather than a philosopher. The facts that will be presented here—many of them familiar to some readers— are arranged so that they point to conclusions. I shall try to say something about Transkei independence (by which I mean *legal* sovereignty) in the larger context of race relations in southern Africa.

Obviously, the movement of Transkei to independence has not been without its interpreters. Indeed, in the middle of 1976 in South Africa journalistic writing about Transkei could only be described as a growth industry. Much of this commentary was highly critical, particularly in English. The international view was reflected in the fact that officially only South Africa (aside from Transkei itself) was represented at Umtata on October 25. All other governments that had received invitations (and they are believed to have been many) were pointedly absent. Instead, 7,000 miles away at the General Assembly of the United Nations in New York, 134 countries marked the day by supporting a resolution (31/6A) declaring Transkei independence "invalid" and prohibiting any future dealings with the new state. No country voted against the resolution, and only the United States abstained.

It seems clear if one examines this criticism that a common premise is that any form of race separation in South Africa is both morally and historically indefensible and no positive answer whatsoever to the awful tensions of the region. Instead, inspired by the prospect (in 1976) of impending political changes in Rhodesia/Zimbabwe and South West Africa/ Namibia, many of the proponents of ignoring Transkei and deprecating its independence make deterministic references to the "tide of history," which they confidently assume will shortly break over white South Africa and in the name of majority rule sweep away all vestiges of institutionalized white privilege and power. A variety of individuals and groups are allied in this view, including a school of social science writing on South Africa that has become well established over the past decade, particularly in Great Britain—the "radical-revisionists," or neo-Marxists. David Yudelman has written that the members of this school

> are committed to revolutionary change: their theory suggests that the inner dynamics of South African industrialization perpetuates racial discrimination and that some external agent must be added to the equation if structural change is to be realized.[1]

Others believe that accumulating pressures short of resolution can ultimately compel South African whites to renounce apartheid/separate development, as, under pressure, Prime Minister Ian Smith of Rhodesia appeared to make fundamental changes in his position in September 1976. From either perspective, Transkei independence is anathema, or at least an irrelevance. And while it is seldom articulated, the presumption seems to be that when fundamental change has come to South Africa, whether peacefully or by revolutionary means, the people of Transkei will somehow dissolve their independent political identification and align themselves with the new ruling groups in the republic. The new Republic of Transkei is thus seen by many of these critics as a temporary phenomenon and Transkei independence as a reversible step.

These prognostications may eventually be shown to be substantially correct. Many well-informed and thoughtful observers believe the probability is high. Indeed, the idea that a violent revolution could come to South Africa is increasingly commonplace, for the revolutionary potential of the situation would appear to be undeniable. Dennis Austin has listed the ingredients of this potential as follows: (1) a conflict of mutually exclusive nationalisms, (2) a reinforcing racial conflict, (3) heightened class tensions paralleling the foregoing, (4) international pressures on South Africa, including the elimination of the former protective ring of

1. David Yudelman, "Industrialization, Race Relations and Change in South Africa: An Ideological and Academic Debate," *African Affairs* 74, no. 294 (January 1975): 94.

buffer states, and (5) loss of white morale.[2] It is an impressive array of forces, all or most of which are thought to be intensifying, suggesting to many individuals an increasingly explosive social mixture in the republic which soon, and perhaps even now, may require only the spark of some specific violent encounter to be ignited. And on the record the capacity of this society to generate such an encounter seems great indeed.

Nonetheless, this book rests on different premises:

• The current political situation in the Republic of South Africa *is* unstable and tends toward greater levels of violence. In time South Africa must find a more stable arrangement; but successful revolution, while possible, is neither inevitable nor perhaps even likely.

• The white South African regime can be expected to respond to pressures on it with higher levels of official coercion directed at its domestic opponents and with measures of accommodation that fall short of simple majority rule. Loosely speaking, these measures will be separatist in character.

• These separatist measures could in time succeed in reducing the legitimate grievances of the oppressed populations in South Africa, opening the way for lower levels of official coercion and more democracy in general.

Of course these measures might also fail to reduce tensions in the region, possibly because they were poorly conceived or did not go far enough. The purpose of this work, then, is to think again about separatism as a means of reducing race conflict in southern Africa. The specific issue I address in these pages is whether the existence of Transkei as an independent state contributes to an increase in racial justice in the region, lessens the chance for racial justice, or is irrelevant to the matter.

In writing this book I have had two marginally overlapping groups of individuals in mind as my primary audience. The

2. Dennis Austin, "White Power: Cohesion without Consensus?" *Government and Opposition* 13, no. 1 (Winter 1978): 22–28.

larger consists of persons in many parts of the world who recognize the special problems posed by multiethnic societies. Crawford Young's recent book, *The Politics of Cultural Pluralism* (1976), is perhaps the leading statement of this concern, but while Young devotes a great deal of attention to Africa within an overall focus substantially limited to the Third World, he makes remarkably few references to South Africa. It seems to me probable that there are some lessons to be learned from Transkei independence that can be applied to generalizations about politics in plural societies as a class of phenomena. In particular it bears on the question why strategies of secession in such a situation succeed or fail.

The second and more specific group of intended readers is exemplified by the professional staff of the Africa Institute in Pretoria (where this writing was begun in late 1976) and includes other persons of similar general orientation and influence, most of whom of course are white and Afrikaans-speaking, in South African society. The justification (if one is needed) for seeking to address these individuals, apart from the fact that some of them are friends, is that they are close to the centers of political power, and I assume therefore that for the foreseeable future how they exert their influence will be of considerable importance. On its face, the willingness of the Pretoria government to divest itself of sovereignty over a portion of its territory the size of Switzerland is an unusual step and deserves to be considered seriously. This I have tried to do, from a personal orientation that is conservative, or at least on the conservative side of center. One value, then, of this work may be that it represents about as sympathetic a reading of their Transkei policies as the whites of South Africa are likely to get from an outsider who presumes to be both objective and informed. Those less well disposed toward white South Africa will, I suspect, see it as lending added weight to such negative judgments as are contained in the chapters that follow, while possibly allowing them to dismiss most of the positive judgments. My hope (and expectation) is that the members of my second group will not just simply reverse this process, accepting the positive observations and ignoring the rest.

Concluding this preface I wish to thank again the many individuals and organizations that have helped me on this project. A fellowship in the Conflict in International Relations program of the Rockefeller Foundation enabled me to go to southern Africa for three months in 1976 and to work full time on my materials for some months after returning. And toward the end of my writing, a visiting fellowship at Yale University's Southern African Research Program, a program made possible by grants from the National Endowment for the Humanities and the Ford Foundation, allowed me to devote full time to it for one semester. Within South Africa I profited from my affiliation with the Institute of African Studies at the University of the Witwatersrand and from the resources of the Africa Institute in Pretoria. I am especially grateful for the assistance of and encouragement by the following persons: W. J. Breytenbach, Jeffrey Butler, Gwendolen Carter, Allie Dubb, Deon and Felicia Fourie, David Hammond-Tooke, Basil Heald, Tom Karis, D. A. Kotze, Patrick Laurence, Theo Malan, Philip Mayer, Schalk and Rona Olckers, Christian Potholm, Arthur Rose, Bruce Stephenson, and David Thomas. My colleagues at Yale— Heribert Adam, Bill Foltz, Hermann Giliomee, Stanley Greenberg, Richard Ralston, and Leonard Thompson—each read some of the manuscript and made important suggestions. Pamela Baldwin at Yale and Ruby Walker at Brown graciously agreed to type the final manuscript. Portions of the book have already appeared in *South Africa International, Plural Societies,* and the *Journal of African Studies,* and I thank the editors of these journals for permission to reprint this material here. Finally, I am grateful to my colleagues in the Department of Political Science at Brown University and to Betsy, Elliot, and Amy Stultz of Barrington, Rhode Island, for their cheerful willingness to take up my normal duties while I was away, twice within the space of one year.

1

SEPARATISM

The problem that one immediately encounters when considering how to bring about racial justice in South Africa is that the simple majoritarian, winner-take-all model of liberal democracy that evolved in Great Britain, and that many in the West see as the sine qua non for social justice anywhere, seems inapplicable to societies such as South Africa that consist of a number of separate subcultures deeply divided from each other. By "inapplicable" I mean that in such a situation liberal democratic institutions are not likely to bring forth liberal democratic results. This conclusion seldom emerges from the contemporary speeches of statesmen, for the normative appeal of such slogans as "one man, one vote" and "majority rule" is irresistible for millions of oppressed, and formerly oppressed, persons, but over the past decade it has become well grounded in the literature of comparative politics. For example, reviewing W. Arthur Lewis's book, *Politics in West Africa,* Sidney Verba wrote in 1967:

> Unlike Europe, where divisions are on economic grounds, the African nations are plural societies in which majoritarian systems of rule will not apply; one group cannot be expected to turn power over to its opponents when they are separated by linguistic and tribal barriers. The various

groups can coexist without the suppression of one by another only if they are protected from each other.[1]

Indeed, Eric Nordlinger, my colleague at Brown University, has concluded that an exclusive reliance on majoritarian institutions and practices in a deeply divided society "does not facilitate conflict regulation, and may even contribute to conflict exacerbation."[2] And similarly, Arend Lijphart has written:

> In practice, majority rule works well when opinions are distributed unimodally and with relatively little spread—in other words, when there is considerable consensus and majority and minority are in fact not very far apart. . . . But, in a political system with clearly separate and potentially hostile population segments, virtually all decisions are perceived as entailing high stakes, and strict majority rule places a strain on the unity and peace of the system.[3]

The obvious challenge in such a situation is to devise a way to protect one group without at the same time opening the way to oppression of another.

Political mechanisms seeming to have this effect have been found and described in the domestic politics of a number of smaller western European countries (that is, Austria, Belgium, Norway, Switzerland, and the Netherlands), giving rise to a conception in the field of comparative politics termed *consociational democracy*. Quoting Verba again, "The main pattern involves violation of the majority principle so that the various subcultures can be protected."[4] Nordlinger, whose study of the problem extended beyond Europe to include both Lebanon and Malaysia, has identified six such "conflict regulating practices" employed in six deeply

1. Sidney Verba, "Some Dilemmas in Comparative Research," *World Politics* 20, no. 1 (1967): 125.
2. Eric A. Nordlinger, *Conflict Regulation in Divided Societies* (Cambridge: Center for International Affairs, Harvard University, 1972), p. 117.
3. Arend Lijphart, *Democracy in Plural Societies: A Comparative Exploration* (New Haven and London: Yale University Press, 1977), p. 28.
4. Verba, "Some Dilemmas in Comparative Research," p. 126.

divided societies having (at least at the time of his examination of them) "open" regimes. The six practices are: (1) a stable governing coalition between or among the political parties, (2) proportional representation of groups in both elective and appointive positions, (3) a mutual veto, (4) purposive depoliticization of sensitive policy areas, (5) compromise, and (6) concession. Two other techniques that Nordlinger chose not to discuss but that are mentioned elsewhere by Robert Dahl as common (if more extreme) ways of dealing with conflict in deeply divided societies are semi-autonomy (or federalism) and secession (or territorial partition).[5] The latter of course is the most radical step in that it attempts to reduce intergroup conflict by taking it out of the arena of domestic politics altogether and placing it in the field of international relations. For Lijphart, territorial partition goes further than mere consociationalism, although federal arrangements could be such a device.

> There are three types of solutions to deal with the political problems of a plural society while maintaining its democratic nature. One is to eliminate or substantially reduce the plural character of the society through assimilation—a method with a low probability of success, especially in the short run. The second is the consociational solution which accepts the plural divisions as the basic building blocks for a stable democratic regime. Especially if the second solution should be very unlikely to succeed or if it was tried and failed, the remaining logical alternative is to reduce the pluralism by dividing the state into two or more separate and more homogeneous states.[6]

Although Crawford Young, for one, has objected to the contention of Alvin Rabushka and Kenneth Shepsle that democratic politics are always incompatible with cultural pluralism, it is generally accepted that the deeper and more bitter the divisions in a society, the greater the infringement of the majoritarian principle that may be required to ensure

5. Robert A. Dahl, ed., *Political Opposition in Western Democracies* (New Haven: Yale University Press, 1966), p. 358.
6. Lijphart, *Democracy in Plural Societies*, pp. 44–45.

that anarchy or the oppression of one group by another does not occur.[7] Doubtless because of an intuitive recognition of this principle, as well as the desperate nature of the situation, thinking within South Africa about humane alternatives to majority rule has tended to focus on racial partition or on federation of several racially defined states, although renewed consideration has recently been given to less drastic modifications of the present system that (some imagine) might produce a similar beneficent result, such as "cantons" and ethnic parliaments. Such thinking is generally referred to as "separatism," since it seeks somehow to separate the various racial groups in South Africa in order to prevent the emergence of an integrated society, which many observers assume would in fact be highly conflictive.

But if territorial partition is in principle a recognized way of trying to resolve certain types of social conflict situations that seem unlikely to yield to simple majoritarian or consociational answers, there has been surprisingly little effort to generalize about how successful partition solutions come to pass. This is especially apparent when one compares the scanty literature on partition with the extensive literature on federalism. Two explanations seem probable. One is normative, the widespread attitude that the dividing up of states is socially retrogressive, as witness the pejorative connotations of the verb "to balkanize." Samuel Huntington's colorful statement of the point seems apt: "The twentieth century bias against political divorce, that is, secession, is just about as strong as the nineteenth century bias against marital divorce."[8] The second explanation lies in the relative absence of cross-national comparative studies of partition. Even a recent volume by Gregory Henderson and two coauthors that presents case studies of the partitioning of Ireland, South Asia, Ruanda-Urundi, and Israel comes to conclusions that are limited, as well as pessimistic. They see little hope that

7. Crawford Young, *The Politics of Cultural Pluralism* (Madison: University of Wisconsin Press, 1976), p. 517. The work by Rabushke and Shepsle referred to is *Politics in Plural Societies: A Theory of Democratic Instability* (Columbus, Ohio: Merrill Publishing Co., 1972), p. 217.
8. Nordlinger, *Conflict Regulation in Divided Societies*, p. vii.

partition has resolved the outstanding problems of these countries, primarily because partition failed "to separate the conflicting communities effectively."[9] When territorial partition has been considered in and for South Africa, the topic has therefore been approached essentially de novo, in isolation from possibly comparable experience elsewhere. In contrast, thinking in South Africa about federal solutions to its dilemmas has not shown similar parochialism.

Some of the separatist ideas that have been discussed for South Africa will be examined now, so that Transkei independence can be evaluated later in the book in terms of the thinking of South Africans themselves and of interested outsiders. I have deliberately excluded, however, ideas emanating from official circles in South Africa and from close allies of the National party government. Far more thought has been given, of course, to partition within than outside official circles, and the government's own program has clearly disappointed some of the proponents of separatism, but that is not my concern here, interesting though it might be if we were analyzing policymaking in South Africa. My intention is rather to evaluate a specific policy outcome, that is, Transkei independence, and the principle followed is the familiar maxim that "no one should be judge in his own cause." Finally, because Transkei independence represents a territorial separation, I will discuss only those separatist ideas that involve a substantial territorial base, namely, partition and federalism. Whatever merits other possible separatist models may offer, they do not seem relevant to the experience of Transkei.

Partition
The idea of partitioning South Africa in order to create a number of racially homogeneous states or, alternatively, states in which the interests of one race would predominate under a

9. Gregory Henderson, Richard Ned Lebow, and John G. Stoessinger, *Divided Nations in a Divided World* (New York: McKay, 1974), p. 442. A brief study of partition that is both normatively favorable to the idea and comparative in its methodology is Norman J. G. Pounds, "History and Geography: A Perspective on Partition," *Journal of International Affairs* 18, no. 2 (1964): 161–72.

democratic system, is an old one. The essence of the conception can be found in the race segregation policies of Prime Minister J. B. M. Hertzog in 1923-24, but Hertzog could not implement his program because of opposition in parliament.[10] The first explicit and extended consideration of partition was probably provided by Professor R. F. Alfred Hoernle, president of the S.A. Institute of Race Relations, in his Phelps-Stokes Lectures at the University of Cape Town in May 1939, reproduced the same year in his book *South African Native Policy and the Liberal Spirit*. Hoernlé concluded that total separation of the races in South Africa was not feasible, largely on economic grounds, though more attention has been paid to his belief that the separation of whites and blacks, each into their own "areas of liberty," could be accepted as a genuinely liberal ideal.[11] Hoernlé's opinion carried considerable weight because of his impeccable liberal credentials. After World War II the idea reappeared in the thinking of a number of Afrikaans scholars at the University of Stellenbosch and at the South African Bureau of Racial Affairs, which they helped to found.[12] From this source, primarily, it penetrated the thinking of some members of the ruling National party after 1948. But to date, the most extensive discussion of racial partition of South Africa by individuals not allied with the regime occurred in the 1960s possibly reflecting a heightened appreciation in those years of the intractability of the racial conflict.

On October 15, 1960, Dr. Jan Graaff, an economist and younger brother of the then leader of the opposition, Sir de Villiers Graaff, suggested partition in a newspaper article in the *Cape Argus* and provided a map depicting his proposal. Reacting to this, Professor Denis V. Cowen of the University of Cape Town discussed partition in a journal article and then, a year later, in his book *Foundations of Freedom*. In

10. Edward A. Tiryakian, "Sociological Realism: Partition for South Africa?" *Social Forces* 46, no. 2 (December 1967): 210.

11. R. F. A. Hoernlé, *South African Native Policy and the Liberal Spirit* (Cape Town: University of Cape Town, 1939), p. 173.

12. See Newell M. Stultz, "The Separatist Challenge to White Domination in South Africa," in Mark Karp ed., *African Dimensions: Essays in Honor of William O. Brown* (Boston: African Studies Center, Boston University, 1975) pp. 99-106.

1964 Colin Legum of the London *Observer* and his wife, Margaret, reviewed the Graaff proposal in *South Africa: Crisis for the West.* A French journalist, Paul Giniewski, urged partition in a book published in Cape Town in 1961. Two years later, a British journalist, John Mander, put forward the idea in *Encounter.* Gill Evans, a former employee of the United Nations, wrote an article entitled "Partition and South Africa's Future" in the *Journal of International Affairs* in 1964. And in the same decade three American scholars entered the debate: Gwendolen Carter, director of the Program of African Studies at Northwestern University, in her 1966 Hoernlé Memorial Lecture in Cape Town, Austin Turk of Indiana University, and Edward Tiryakian of Duke University, each in articles in *Social Forces* in 1967. Apparently only two such pieces were published between 1970 and 1978. One was the section on "the practical possibilities of partition" appearing in the report of the political commission of the Study Project on Christianity in Apartheid Society (SPRO-CAS), entitled *South Africa's Political Alternatives.* The second was an article in the July 1976 issue of *Aussenpolitik,* written by two German scholars, Jurgen Blenck and Klaus von der Ropp, under the title, "Republic of South Africa: Partition a Solution?"[13]

13. Denis Victor Cowen, *The Foundations of Freedom with Special Reference to Southern Africa* (Cape Town: Oxford University Press, 1971), p. 71. The earlier piece by Cowen is entitled "Constitution-Making for a Democracy: An Alternative to Apartheid," *Optima,* supplement to vol. 10, no. 1 (March 1960). See especially p. 5. Colin and Margaret Legum, *South Africa: Crisis for the West* (New York: Praeger, 1964), pp. 221–26. Paul Giniewski, *Bantustans: A Trek Towards the Future* (Cape Town: Human & Rousseau, 1961), pp. 220–26. John Mander, "South Africa: Revolution or Partition?" *Encounter* 21, no. 4 (October 1963): 11–20. Gill Evans, "Partition and South Africa's Future," *Journal of International Affairs* 18, no. 2 (1964): 241–52. Gwendolen M. Carter, *Separate Development: The Challenge of the Transkei* (Johannesburg: S.A. Institute of Race Relations, 1966), pp. 14–16. Austin T. Turk, "The Futures of South Africa," *Social Forces* 45, no. 3 (March 1967): 402–12. Edward A. Tiryakian, "Sociological Realism." Peter Randall, ed., *South Africa's Political Alternatives* (Johannesburg: Ravan Press, 1973), pp. 113–17. Jurgan Blenck and Klaus von der Ropp, "Republic of South Africa: Partition a Solution?" *Aussenpolitik* 27, no. 3 (October 1976): 310–27.

The dozen pieces cited diverge on key points. For example, Graaff, Giniewski, Tiryakian, Mander, Blenck and von der Ropp were sympathetic to a partition solution, whereas Hoernlé, Gill, Cowen, the Legums, SPRO-CAS, and Turk doubted that it was practicable. Carter believed that a partition solution meeting certain criteria could succeed, but she seemed to prefer integration. Yet allowing for different emphases, there are interesting areas of substantial agreement. It should be noted, however, that, except for the SPRO-CAS report, none of the pieces in this literature built upon any of the earlier contributions, although some made reference to others. Thus, not only has the idea of racial partition been approached without consideration of possibly comparable experience in other parts of the world, but it has also tended to be discussed by individuals working and thinking independently of each other. It would be incorrect therefore to speak of a separat'st school of thought (outside official circles in South Africa of course).

Land area. Except for Giniewski, for whom partition meant implementation of the Bantustan program, though defined somewhat more generously from the African point of view, all the writers I have mentioned understood partition to be a racial division of South Africa far more radical than current official plans.[14] Graaff suggested that Africans should

14. Under the government's so-called Bantustan program (under which Transkei became independent), the African reserve areas of South Africa—rural and tribal lands comprising (with Transkei) 13 percent of the total surface area of the republic—were divided in 1959 along ethnic lines into eight (later ten) "homelands," each intended to have political autonomy with the option of becoming constitutionally fully independent in time. Concurrently the remainder of the country was in effect defined as a white homeland, minus such "group areas" as have been established for the 2,306,000 coloureds (persons of mixed blood) and the 709,000 Asians who live alongside the 4,160,000 whites in South Africa (June 1974 figures). Here, in so-called white South Africa (or, more accurately, white-claimed South Africa), official policy holds that Africans (numbering altogether 17,745,000 in 1974), being away from their homelands, are properly rightless aliens whose presence is justified only so long as they are meeting needs of the white community.

control 40 percent of the surface area of the republic (before Transkei independence). This would be approximately three times the amount of land reserved for African use under the 1936 Native Trust and Land Act, which the government now calls the "last word" in this matter. Blenck and von der Ropp projected a fifty-fifty division of the surface area between blacks and whites, but the black portion in their scheme now accounts for 74.7 percent of the gross domestic product of South Africa. Cowen stated, "the whites might be lucky to keep [just] the Western Province."[15] No support was given by anyone to the proposition that Pretoria's reservation of 87 percent of the surface area of the country to the non-African 29 percent of the population was equitable, realistic, or ultimately politically defensible.

A division of all resources. Giniewski expressed the opinion that "in a partitioned South Africa the jewels will remain in the hands of the Whites: the mines, the ports, the towns." Accordingly, he continued, "the Blacks must receive compensation for this in the form of the initial capital for the industrialization of the reserves."[16] All of the others who addressed this point disagreed profoundly and argued instead that every state resulting from partition, white and black alike, should already have some industry, a diversified economy, natural resources, farmland, cities, a coastline, port facilities, reasonable boundaries, and internal communications relevant to its needs. In short, partition should entail a comprehensive division of the wealth and resources of the country, not just of the land, and the creation of complete and reasonably modern states. In particular, Africans should not be "pushed back into . . . an artificial perpetuation of 'primitive' ways" (Hoernlé) or "shut off from the world outside and from each other" (Carter).[17]

Three authors provided actual maps showing how a partitioned South Africa might look. Regarding the placement of

15. Cowen, *Foundations of Freedom*, p. 72.
16. Giniewski, *Bantustans*, p. 226.
17. Hoernle, *South African Native Policy*, p. 172; Carter, *Separate Development*, p. 14.

cities, for example, Graaff's map allocated Durban and Pietermaritzburg to the Africans and left the status of East London undecided. Tiryakian proposed all three as African-controlled cities and added Johannesburg and the entire western Witwatersrand, but not Pretoria. The map prepared by Blenck and von der Ropp reserved to the whites just four of the nine largest municipalities in the republic: Cape Town, Port Elizabeth, Bloemfontein, and Kimberley. Carter's map, which was verbal, included a brief but novel suggestion for the future of the Witwatersrand area: that its substantial wealth not be divided, but rather shared by the new black and white states of the region. In 1976 the essence of this idea was greatly elaborated with respect to the Pretoria-Witwatersrand-Vereeniging area in a paper written by Erich Leistner of the Africa Institute in Pretoria.[18] But whatever the specific plan, partition would clearly involve sweeping material sacrifices on the part of whites, which was the principal reason why Cowen and the Legums suspected the whites of South Africa could never agree to it.

Economic viability. A point of particular significance to several commentators is that any African state resulting from partition should be economically viable, that is, capable of subsisting without the aid of the whites. For Hoernle this meant that no Africans should have to find employment in the white areas: they should be able to work and prosper in the area of their permanent residence. And for Blenck and von der Ropp it meant that economic dealings between the black and white states should not constitute an "imperialistic relationship of dependency" of the former upon the latter.[19] Such a situation would produce race conflict, they believed, and defeat the purpose of partition. What they proposed, therefore, was the economic disentanglement of the races, which clearly could be accomplished only as a result of massive (and presumably costly) reorganization of the present economy. Hoernlé, Evans, and Turk took this to be virtually impossible.

18. Erich Leistner, "Towards a New Order in South Africa," *Africa Institute Bulletin* 14, nos. 7 and 8 (1976): 266–67.
19. Blenck and von der Ropp, "Partition a Solution?" p. 318.

Nonracialism. For Hoernlé, partition would involve the "total separation" of Africans and whites in a territorial sense.[20] Hence, race discrimination as a matter of daily human relations would simply disappear. In contrast, both Graaff and Tiryakian thought that after partition there would be some Africans remaining in the white areas and vice versa. Moreover, each of the writers who mentioned the coloureds (persons of mixed blood) assumed that they should remain with the whites. Blenck and von der Ropp left the Asians with the whites as well, although 75 percent of the Asians would have to leave their homes to accomplish this. They based this unusual recommendation on the exclusion of Asians from Uganda and Malawi and the record of tense Asian-African relations in South Africa. Hence for most of these observers the future white state would in fact have a multiracial population, and this would be true to a lesser degree of the African state or states as well. Nevertheless, having projected through partition the establishment of states in which the interests of either Africans or whites could naturally (that is, democratically) predominate, Tiryakian and Carter anticipated, or perhaps required (if partition was to be taken seriously), the establishment of nonracial policies everywhere. Under Graaff's plan, however, whites would not be a majority of the total population of the "white" state. Accordingly, he would have extended the vote to coloureds living in the "white" state, but not to the 3.5 million Africans there.

Population transfers. Graaff drew his partition lines so as to require as little in the way of shifts of population as possible. The result, as we have just seen, was a "white" state in which whites were a minority of the total population and continued an official policy of political discrimination against Africans. Most of the other writers were unwilling to pay this price. Accordingly, most partition plans assumed the necessity for some transfers of population, but only Tiryakian, Evans, and SPRO-CAS dealt with the point directly, and then only briefly. Furthermore, none discussed the complicated

20. Hoernlé, *South African Native Policy*, p. 169.

issue of how a major metropolitan area—Durban or Johannesburg, for example—might pass from white control to black
control. Critical issues of the logistics of partition were
clearly ignored.

Few black states. The general expectation was that partition would produce a single white state, but the number of
projected black states differed. Giniewski anticipated six,
Turk suggested several, and Mander envisioned two. However,
Graaff, Tiryakian, and Blenck and von der Ropp foresaw one
black state only, although Tiryakian suggested it might be a
federal republic incorporating Lesotho and Swaziland. Cowen
and the Legums, taking the Graaff plan as the basis for their
discussions, appeared to contemplate a simple division of
South Africa into two racially defined countries.

Blenck and von der Ropp stressed the advantage of the
two-state model (one black, one white). A single large black
state would have more political power and greater economic
viability than any of several smaller ones, and it would be
more clearly the equal of its neighboring white state. Blenck
and von der Ropp believed that this would contribute to the
stability of the region.

The need for consensus. Most of the writers we are dealing
with acknowledged the importance of marshaling broad
political support for partition and the difficulty of doing so.
Turk and the Legums considered the possibility that partition might be imposed on an unwilling South Africa from the
outside and rejected this as extremely unlikely. But Cowen
and Hoernlé doubted that the whites in South Africa would
be able to accept the material sacrifices that a fair partition
would necessarily entail. Yet, in Cowen's words, "unless the
partition is genuinely fair, what real prospects are there for
peaceful co-existence between the white and the non-white
territories?"[21] Tiryakian also warned that partition would be
"doomed were it defined by Africans as a European scheme
to deprive the blacks of what is [rightfully] theirs."[22]
Mander believed that the key issue was whether or not parti-

21. Cowen, *Foundations of Freedom,* p. 71.
22. Tiryakian, "Sociological Realism," p. 215.

tion could be made acceptable to African nationalists, and Carter underlined the need for negotiations involving "representative national as well as local leaders of the groups concerned."[23] Clearly she was thinking of those African leaders who were banned, imprisoned, or in exile. The Legums stated flatly that partition would not work in South Africa, because "no section of the population wants it," a view with which Evans emphatically concurred.[24]

An alternative to violence. But will not conceptions of individual and group self-interest change with altered circumstances? There were several suggestions that the political acceptability of partition could increase if the alternative was clearly seen to be widespread and interminable violence. SPRO-CAS, for example, concluded that although the dominant white government would never consider partition of its own accord, "it is conceivable that it could be adopted as a desperate measure in an extreme impasse."[25] Indeed, many of the writers agreed that South Africans of all colors, and probably the West as well, could be expected to prefer an equitable partition of South Africa to a lengthy race war.

From this review, we can see that those who have written on partition seem in essential agreement on what the goal should be, at least from the standpoint of satisfying African interests. Most believed that, to succeed, partition should produce one or at most two or three African-controlled states, which together should cover something like half (or more) of the surface area of the republic (before Transkei independence). I shall describe one such state, which for convenience I will call Azania. (In fact this is the name suggested by the banned Pan Africanist Congress for the entire Republic of South Africa after its projected "liberation" from white minority rule.) The expectation, then, has been that Azania should be a large state possessing substantial industry, a prosperous and diversified economy, natural resources including both farmland and mineral wealth, major urban areas, outlets to the sea, compact territory and reasonable boundaries, and

23. Carter, *Separate Development*, p. 14.
24. Legum and Legum, *South Africa: Crisis for the West*, p. 222.
25. Randall, *South Africa's Political Alternatives*, pp. 115–16.

an internal infrastructure appropriate to its needs. Further, it has been supposed that Azania's economy should be minimally dependent on white South Africa, implying a virtual cessation of migratory labor. Politically, Azania could be a federal or a unitary system, but it should not be dominated by African traditionalists, that is, chiefs. What has certainly been envisaged is an African nationalist regime on the pattern of Zambia or Kenya, although probably not Tanzania or Mozambique. Whether or not such a regime would be democratic in the liberal Western sense, it has been considered critical that the initial founding of Azania should be an undeniably popular step among Africans. Hence some sort of referendum on the partition question has been assumed.

Federalism
Unlike some of the opponents of partition whose position has ultimately rested, it seems, on normative grounds, none of the twelve authors I have just discussed emphasized any objection to partition based on moral or philosophical principles. Their problems with partition have not been problems of principle but problems of practicality, and in this respect they are representative of a broad spectrum of opinion. Accordingly, one finds numerous efforts to devise separatist solutions for South Africa that do not require, for example, as partition would, the movement of tens of thousands of persons across newly drawn boundaries or the disintegration of the South African economy. Calls for a federal solution have been frequent. Indeed, in the middle of the 1970s both of the opposition parties in the South African Parliament were committed to their own form of federalism for the republic as a means of dealing with race tensions, and at different times several of the homeland leaders have seemed to favor a federal solution as well.

The meaning typically assigned to federalism is the familar one—a system of government in which a rigid constitution divides legislative and executive authority between a central government and a number of unit governments. The presumption of most commentators is that in South Africa a federal system should include a bill of rights that would eliminate racial discrimination, certainly in all matters of fed-

eral concern. Obviously, there are other details in the arrangement to be worked out as well. One on which there are substantive differences that may be relevant here concerns the
number and particularly the character of the constituent
units of a federation. In the program of the now defunct
United party, for example, the entities that were to be joined
federally were South Africa's four racial communities, not
regions or pieces of territory. The proposal of the Progressive
Federal party (formerly the Progressive Reform party) is
more conventional. It anticipates a federation of self-
governing states. The number of such states is unspecified,
but it is clear the party expects some of them would be
African homelands that have not chosen independence.

This last proposal resembles ideas put forward in 1971 by
Leo Marquard in *A Federation of Southern Africa*. To date
this has clearly been the definitive study of the problem,
albeit from a profederalism point of view. Marquard made
the point that "federation is not advisable where there is too
great a difference in economic strength among the federating
units,"[26] and he therefore suggested dividing South Africa
into eleven regions, none of which would be disproportion-
ately powerful. This division would also enable most of the
regions to have a particular ethnic character, though not a
culturally homogeneous population. The eleven regions could
then federate, and when this had been done Lesotho, Swaziland, Botswana, and Namibia might come in as well.

Although he did not stress the point, perhaps deliberately
in order not to arouse white fears, Marquard seemed to suggest that the white heartland of South Africa itself ought to
be broken up politically. André du Toit of Stellenbosch University has pointed to the threat that any such proposal has
for the forces of Afrikaner nationalism, yet he too appeared
to find the step a prerequisite to successful federation. In his
1974 Maurice Webb Memorial Lectures on federalism given in
Durban, du Toit said:

> A political arrangement between the Republican govern-
> ment as representative of a unified White group, as the

26. Leo Marquard, *A Federation of Southern Africa* (London:
Oxford University Press, 1971), p. 70.

"senior partner", and a series of fragmented Black groups represented by the Bantustan governments, as very much "junior partners", would, whatever else one might think of its viability, certainly not constitute a federation in any recognizable sense. A political alliance between, on the one hand, a state with an overwhelming preponderance in power and resources and, on the other, a number of smaller satellites would approach more nearly to some species of empire.[27]

A somewhat different formulation of a federal future for South Africa was offered by Chief Gatsha Buthelezi of KwaZulu in his 1974 Hoernlé Memorial Lecture in Cape Town. This speech has been referred to often since then, although in fact its ideas are remarkably similar to a proposal made by Jordan K. Ngubane, a prominent African politician and journalist, eleven years earlier in a book published in the United States. Buthelezi suggested a federation of three different types of states. In one the interests of an African ethnic group would be dominant. Clearly he had the larger African homelands in mind. A second type would be states in which the interests of whites would prevail. (Ngubane had proposed two types of white states, one Afrikaner-dominated and the other British-dominated.) And the third would be states that are multiethnic, in which the interests of no group would be allowed to dominate.[28] Both Buthelezi and Marquard emphasized that the boundaries of the states of a federation, in addition to all other details, could not be worked out by the whites and then simply imposed upon everyone else. These decisions require, rather, prolonged discussion and bargaining involving all parties, as well as the advice of experts.

27. André du Toit, "Federalism and Political Change in S.A." Part 2. "How can a Federation of Southern Africa come about?" Maurice Webb Memorial Lecture (1974), typescript, p. 14.
28. Chief Gatsha Buthelezi, *White and Black Nationalism, Ethnicity and the Future of the Homelands* (Johannesburg: S.A. Institute of Race Relations, 1974), p. 14. Jordan K. Ngubane, *An African Explains Apartheid* (New York: Praeger, 1963), pp. 220–32.

We are now in a position to consider whether the establishment in 1976 of an independent Republic of Transkei was consistent or inconsistent with the two separatist solutions to South Africa's conflict that we have just discussed—partition and federation. In area, Transkei is about 16,600 square miles. It is thus larger than Switzerland or the Netherlands or, moving to the other side of the Atlantic, the combined area of the American states of Connecticut, Rhode Island, and Massachusetts. Still, it was only 3.51 percent of the surface area of the former republic. Its resident black population was 11.5 percent of all blacks in the former republic. Obviously, Transkei independence could be at best only the beginning of the process of partition or federation. I assume that it *is* a prototype, a representative sample of a larger set of possibilities.

But in one respect, at least, Transkei is clearly *not* representative. Except for the Herschel and Umzimkulu districts, which are geographically separated from the rest, Transkei is a large and compact territory. In contrast, when current plans for the consolidation of the other African homelands have been completed, KwaZulu, for example, will still consist of ten pieces of land. Bophuthatswana, which became independent on December 6, 1977, has seven parts. Further consolidation of the homelands is clearly required if either partition or federation (as they have been described here) is to be taken seriously, and this conclusion does not arise from a focus exclusively on Transkei. A second assumption, namely, that either partition or federation might be arrived at incrementally, one step at a time, rather than in consequence of a single sweeping realignment, will be discussed in chapter 6.

The book is organized first around three questions—a chapter being devoted to each—that summarize the main issues. Does Transkei independence provide a reasonable and practicable division of the resources of South Africa? Did the decision-making process that led to Transkei independence legitimate it? And does Transkei independence in fact eliminate racial discrimination and oppression, that is, is it a "liberating" step? I then review and analyze events after independence before turning to conclusions and an afterword.

2

TRANSKEI'S SHARE

Until February 1977, when Transkei Airways established regular air service between the new K. D. Matanzima Airport outside Umtata and Johannesburg, four hundred miles to the north, most overseas visitors entered Transkei by road from the southwest, coming from the port city of East London (population 120,000). About thirty-five miles from East London the road descends to the floor of a deep and rocky gorge whose sides are dotted by thousands of aloes, standing like frozen infantrymen from some long-forgotten war. At the bottom there is a river that seems too quiet to have carried away so much stone. This is the Great Kei, flowing southeasterly toward the Indian Ocean, twenty-eight miles away. The name is a Khoikhoi (Hottentot) word meaning "sand water" and has been applied to the Ciskei on the river's western bank and to the Transkei on its eastern side. Once across a low bridge one has left South Africa and is in Africa's fiftieth state. Some individuals of course choose to deny this, but if they wish to enter the territory they too must deal with the representatives of the Umtata government at the border. Whatever the standing of Transkei in the world-at-large, once across the Kei River the Transkei state is an unavoidable fact.

In this chapter I will inventory the resources that Transkei possessed at the time of its independence. It seems necessary to do this because separatism in both the forms described involves a racial division of the common South African estate. Here the question arises, What is Transkei's share? And because throughout this discussion of Transkei, issues of equity and social justice are never far away, I will, whenever possible, attempt to approach this material from a comparative point of view, comparing Transkei with so-called white South Africa and with black states elsewhere on the continent.

Citizenship

First I must inquire who the people are who are the recipients of Transkei's share of the common South African estate? Who are the Transkeians? The answer to this straightforward question immediately embroils one in Transkei constitutional law. Since October 26, 1976, when it was passed by the new National Assembly in Umtata, the basic law has been the Republic of Transkei Constitution Act, No. 1, of 1976. In terms of section 57 of this document, three categories of persons are automatically Transkei citizens:

1. All persons born within Transkei on or after October 26, 1976. There are a few trivial exceptions, for example, children of accredited diplomats.

2. All persons born outside Transkei on or after October 26, 1976, to fathers who at the time are themselves Transkei citizens. (Special provision is made for adopted children.)

3. All persons who were Transkei citizens immediately before independence, that is, on October 25, 1976.

But who were the citizens of Transkei immediately before independence? Here the working law is the Transkei Constitution Act, No. 48, of 1963, passed by the South African Parliament in Cape Town. Section 7, paragraph 2, of this act declares the following classes of persons to be Transkei citizens:

1. All Africans born in Transkei.

2. All Africans resident within Transkei for at least five years.

3. Every Xhosa-speaking African in South Africa, except for those persons who belong to, or fall under, the jurisdiction of another Bantu homeland.

4. Every Sotho-speaking African in South Africa who is a member of, or derived from, any of the Sotho-speaking tribes in Transkei.

At the time of the last complete census in 1970, there appear to have been approximately 3,110,000 persons who qualified as Transkei citizens under the 1963 constitution, but of this number only 1,728,240 were found to be actually living within the territory. Where were the others? The Bureau of Economic Research re Bantu Development (Benbo, from the name in Afrikaans) in Pretoria estimates that in the early 1970s there were perhaps 350,000 Africans from Transkei who were at any time temporarily absent in the so-called white areas of the republic, or the white-claimed areas, where they were employed as migrant workers. The remainder, 1,032,000 individuals with Transkei citizenship, were absent from the territory *permanently,* 97 percent being in the white-claimed areas.[1] (The others were scattered among different African homelands.) Most of the Transkeians in the white-claimed areas were in the cities, where by virtue of having been born there or the longevity of their employment (ten years consecutively for one employer or fifteen years among several), they had established the right to remain under section 10 of the Bantu (Urban Areas) Consolidation Act of 1945. Mayer writes that these are the only blacks in the cities "legally entitled to have their family staying with them. They are not liable to be 'endorsed out' if they merely change jobs, or fall out of work for a time, but only if they fall foul of the authorities."[2] Between 1960 and 1970, the black population within Transkei increased by about 20 per-

1. *Transkei: Economic Revue, 1975* (Pretoria: Bureau for Economic Research Re Bantu Development, 1975), p. 11. Following common usage, I employ "republic" to refer to the Republic of South Africa, although Transkei is also officially designated as a republic.

2. Philip Mayer, "Class, Status, and Ethnicity as Perceived by Johannesburg Africans," in Leonard Thompson and Jeffrey Butler, eds., *Change in Contemporary South Africa* (Berkeley and Los Angeles: University of California Press, 1975), p. 144.

cent, while the number of Transkei citizens outside the territory doubtless increased at a somewhat faster rate. On October 26, 1976, therefore, a conservative estimate of the Transkei citizenry would have been that shown in the table.

Estimated Transkei Citizenry, October 1976

Persons continually resident within Transkei	1,935,000
Migrant workers absent temporarily	370,000
Citizens permanently absent from Transkei	1,155,000
TOTAL	3,460,000

The startling conclusion is that at independence exactly one-third of all the citizens of the new state were living permanently elsewhere, nearly all in the white areas of South Africa. The physical separation of Transkeians from the rest of South Africa has thus fallen far short of their legal separation, and whatever the endowment of Transkei, it can have little meaning for one in three Transkeians.

For his part, the new prime minister of Transkei, Paramount Chief Kaiser Daliwonga Matanzima, and his political colleagues heatedly denied during the months before independence that the 1,155,000 individuals mentioned who live permanently outside Transkei were about to have citizenship in the new state thrust upon them. He repeatedly stated publicly that only those Xhosa-speakers outside Transkei who applied for Transkei citizenship would be recognized as citizens, and in his "Address to the Nation" only moments after midnight on October 26, Matanzima reiterated his belief that the people of Transkei are the individuals (including the migrant workers) who live within its borders. On this important occasion, with the republican state president and two members of the South African cabinet looking on, Prime Minister Matanzima referred to Transkeians in the white-claimed areas of the republic as follows:

> It is our view, however, that apart from migratory workers, the millions of Blacks in the Republic of South Africa constitute a permanent society of that country especially as they are now purchasing their own properties in their residential areas. We believe that, of Transkeians resident in the Republic, an insignificant number will wish to return

to Transkei. Their interest in the domestic politics of
Transkei may be expected gradually to wane and increas-
ingly to become comparable with that of say, South
African Jews in the affairs of Israel or resident aliens from
Europe in the internal politics of their old countries.[3]

Matanzima thus appeared to believe that the question of
the citizenship of Transkeians in the white-claimed areas is
not governed by section 57 of the 1976 Transkei Constitution, but is inferable from the next section, section 58. Here
provision is made for individuals to acquire Transkei citizenship through *voluntary* application and registration, and sub-
section (b) refers explicitly in this regard to an application
from a person "who is predominantly Xhosa-speaking or
Sotho-speaking and is a member of or descended from, or
ethnically, culturally or otherwise associated with any tribe
resident in any [Transkei] district." Indeed, this note of
voluntarism was missing from an earlier draft of the constitution and was only inserted in July 1976 when the Transkei
Legislative Assembly (TLA) reviewed the document for the
last time. Thereafter, Matanzima asserted that all such individuals living beyond Transkei's borders who declined to
apply for Transkei citizenship would still be South African
citizens and not Transkei citizens at all. But concurrently
competent legal opinion in Cape Town and just about all students of Transkei affairs concluded that Matanzima had
somehow misinterpreted section 58(b), which in its final
form they understood to cover only a handful of individuals,
essentially Africans of uncertain ethnicity, so-called border-
line cases. These observers contended that the overwhelming
majority of Transkeians outside Transkei *were* covered by
section 57 of the new constitution and thus would become
citizens of the new Republic of Transkei on October 26, 1976,
whether they wished to or not.[4] Certainly this situation was

3. Kaiser D. Matanzima, *Address to the Nation on the Occasion of
the Declaration of Independence, 26 October 1976*, p. 5.

4. R. M. Marais, S.C., rendered the legal opinion on June 3, 1976,
which was entitled "In Re Transkei Independence." Views differ on
who solicited this opinion (some say the Black Sash organization), but
there is no doubt it was made available to Chief Matanzima well before
October 26.

assumed in the Status of Transkei Act, which the South African Parliament in Cape Town passed in June 1976. In terms of paragraph 6 of this act, all citizens of Transkei under any law at the time of independence became citizens of the new state automatically, and concurrently ceased to be South African citizens. The idea of joint citizenship was thus excluded.

On October 26, therefore, the citizenship of a minimum of one million "Transkeians" permanently living in the white-claimed areas of the republic, some of whom have never been in Transkei, was anomalous, or at least confused. In time the government of the new state may find it expedient to take steps formally to divest itself of any responsibility for the so-called urban Xhosa, except of course for those persons who do decide to take out Transkei citizenship.[5] One can imagine such a step being taken should Pretoria attempt to deport to the new state numbers of unwanted or unemployable Africans. Indeed, I guessed (wrongly as it turned out) that Matanzima might seek to amend section 57 of the Transkei Constitution in order to produce this clarification at the time the new Transkei National Assembly enacted it on October 26, so that responsibility for making the urban Xhosa stateless (the probable result) would rest clearly on the shoulders of Pretoria rather than of Umtata. But Matanzima declined the opportunity to confront white South Africa on this occasion, although to have done so might have won for Transkei needed international sympathy and respect and have increased the moral case for its existence. Instead, he appeared content to ignore or merely deny the seeming contradiction between his own rhetoric and the language of the Transkei Constitution.

5. The words *urban Xhosa* refer in common usage to Transkei citizens who live permanently outside Transkei. The designation is, however, a misnomer for several reasons. Not all these persons live in cities, and there are more than 400,000 Xhosa speakers in the cities who are Ciskeians and not Transkei citizens at all. Moreover, not all Transkei citizens outside the new state are Xhosa-speaking. A small minority speak Sotho or Zulu. It would be less confusing perhaps to refer to the urban Xhosa as *urban Transkeians,* or *nonresident Transkeians,* but this would suggest the point that is being challenged, namely, that these individuals are in fact Transkeians.

Of course Pretoria does not agree that the legal position of the urban Xhosa is anomalous. On November 7, 1976, for example, Prime Minister John Vorster appearing on the American television news program, "Face the Nation," likened these persons to the citizens of Lesotho, who also work in the republic. But this analogy is faulty. The Lesotho citizens, perhaps 200,000 persons, are migrants who are away from Lesotho only temporarily. They are equivalent to the 350,000 migrant workers from Transkei previously mentioned. There is no equivalent in the case of Lesotho to the 1,155,000 Transkei citizens who are permanently resident in the republic. Basotho, who might have constituted such a population, were left in the republic as citizens of South Africa when Lesotho became independent in 1966. Indeed, it is probably the belated assignment of these persons to the small Basotho-QwaQwa homeland in the republic that creates the extraordinary situation in which less than 2 percent of the citizens of that homeland actually live within it.

Later in this chapter I will review economic data that lead irresistibly to the conclusion that Transkeians in the urban areas, save for the migrant workers, can never be supported in Transkei. I take it as axiomatic, therefore, that the urban Xhosa are permanently divorced from the life of Transkei, and that the resources of Transkei, be they meager or abundant, do not affect their sense of political well-being. The destiny of the urban Xhosa is where they live—in the cities, notwithstanding their Transkeian citizenship. Accordingly, the recipients of "Transkei's share" are defined as those persons who live within Transkei (including a small percentage of migrant workers), and only those persons. The attitude of the Pretoria government toward the urban Xhosa is clearly unrealistic and I assume will have to change in time, by one means or another.

There is one other point regarding Transkei independence. Under the 1963 Transkei Constitution only Africans could qualify for Transkei citizenship, and for some years thereafter it appeared that the policy of the Transkei government after independence would be to restrict the rights of whites and other non-Africans in the territory, a policy of reverse apartheid. For example, in 1971, George Matanzima, minister of justice and brother of the chief minister (as the position was then named), declared that whites living in an independent Transkei would suffer the same disabilities as Africans living in the republic; Transkei would not abandon apartheid (against whites) until it was also abandoned (against blacks) in South Africa.[6] By 1975, however, the prospective policy had changed and the chief minister was assuring one and all that Transkei would be developed as a nonracial state. And pursuant to this pledge, the 1976 Transkei Constitution, section 58(a), permits *any* South African adult (other than a prohibited immigrant) who has lived in the territory for five years to apply for citizenship. At the time of the 1970 census, 10,097 whites, 7,645 coloureds, and just ten Asians were found to be living in Transkei. They constituted less than 1 percent of the de facto population of Transkei, and many of them may not remain as permanent residents after independence. Indeed, seven months after independence it was reported in the Coloured Persons' Representatives Council in Cape Town that at least twenty coloured families had fled Transkei to escape intimidation by local Africans, prompting Transkei Foreign Minister Digby Koyana to promise firm government action against anyone found harassing any section of the population.[7] Those non-Africans who do remain, however, will also be recipients of Transkei's share, at least in principle.

Assets and liabilities
As previously noted, Transkei is bigger in surface area than either Switzerland or the Netherlands. In continental African terms, Transkei is larger than Swaziland, Lesotho, Burundi, Rwanda, Gambia, Equatorial Guinea, and Guinea Bissau. Of these, only Burundi and Rwanda have a larger population than Transkei's, which in fact is larger than the populations of thirteen independent African states. Relating these two variables to each other, we find that population density in Transkei (44.6 persons per square kilometer in 1970) is

6. *The Star,* April 30, 1971.
7. *Daily Dispatch,* June 11, 1977.

higher than that for most other countries in the region, and twice that for South Africa as a whole. This comes as a surprise, for entering the territory from the southwest, one has the impression of rugged and quiet beauty, and save for occasional passing vehicles, an absence of people. The actual population density of Transkei is disguised because less than 3 percent of the resident population is urbanized, a lower percentage than for just about all African countries for which data are available. In fact, no large municipal area lies within Transkei. Its largest town is the capital, Umtata, whose population at independence was under 30,000 persons, and the only other center of consequence is Butterworth, with a population in 1976 of about 20,000 persons.

In addition to the size of its area and population, the following assets of Transkei are noteworthy:

• In 1970, 95 percent of the resident black population of Transkei belonged to twelve tribes that are classified as Cape Nguni, a subdivision of one of the four major divisions of Bantu-speaking tribes in South Africa. There were also 21,000 Zulus in Transkei in the northeast and 60,000 South Sotho in the northwest along the Lesotho border. The Cape Nguni tribes are often referred to as the Xhosa, but this is not strictly correct, anthropologically speaking. Only one of them carries this name, but all twelve speak a dialect of the Xhosa language, which is obviously the basis for the convention, which I, too, shall follow. Although each of the Xhosa-speaking tribes has its own customs and identity, Hammond-Tooke reports that Cape Nguni culture exhibits a "remarkable uniformity."[8] The neighboring Ciskei to the southwest is also Xhosa-speaking, and it would seem both natural and desirable that both Transkei and the Ciskei, together with the intervening white farmlands and the port city of East London, should eventually be joined. But for now, notwithstanding some irredentist sentiment among the 60,000 Sotho of northern Transkei who agitated vainly shortly before independence to be allowed to join another Sotho-speaking

8. Gwendolen M. Carter, Thomas Karis, and Newell M. Stultz, *South Africa's Transkei: The Politics of Domestic Colonialism* (Evanston: Northwestern University Press, 1967), p. 81.

homeland, *Transkei enjoys a cultural homogeneity that is usual among contemporary African states.*

• The Cape Nguni migrated into this region before A.D. 700, and, as far as is known, they were its first inhabitants. Quoting Hammond-Tooke again, "The area of the modern Transkei coincides almost exactly with the traditional country of the Cape Nguni, occupied before contact with the White farmers."[9] That contact came during the last half of the eighteenth century, and during the next century the policy of the colonial government in Cape Town, 700 miles to the west, was to try to keep the white farmers and the African tribesmen separated, an early form of apartheid. To this day the area just west of Transkei is called Border. But this policy failed and open conflicts broke out periodically between the two groups of pastoralists; these conflicts are known as the nine Kaffir Wars, and they occurred between 1779 and 1878. The territory called Transkei resulted from a series of territorial annexations by the Cape government that began in 1877 and were completed in 1894, after which it was treated as an African reserve. (Earlier, in 1871, Basutoland, now Lesotho, had similarly been annexed to the Cape Colony, but the latter found this responsibility an administrative and financial burden, and in 1884 control was transferred to a reluctant Great Britain.) In 1903 a chief magistrate was established for the region as a whole, now known as the United Transkeian Territories, with his seat at Umtata. A federated general council for the entire area (an early legislature) was created in 1931. Two points are thus clear: *The people of Transkei possess a historic claim to the territory of the new state,* which (aside from the non-African 1 percent of the population) they have never shared with others. And by the standards of contemporary Africa, *Transkei has existed as a recognizable political entity for a comparatively long period.*

• Thirteen years separated the attainment of internal "self-government" by Transkei in 1963 and independence in 1976, far longer than comparable periods in most African countries. In Lesotho, for example, less than two years elapsed between

9. Ibid.

the achievement of responsible government in 1965 and independence on October 4, 1966. Comparatively speaking, *the Transkei government at independence was an experienced government.* To be sure, on the eve of independence South African whites still filled 2.5 percent of all civil service positions in Transkei (and these mainly top positions), but this figure was down from 18.6 percent in 1963.[10]

A list of Transkei's liabilities, is, however, formidable.

● The territory's natural resources are exceedingly limited, being primarily good (but poorly used) agricultural lands, spectacular scenery, a mild climate, and cheap labor. The region is well watered, and one-fifth of the surface area is arable, most of which (86.5 percent) is, in fact, farmed. However, only about 11 percent of the land is sufficiently flat to allow mechanized farming. Much of the remaining land is suitable for grazing or timber, but because of the value the traditional African culture places on the possession of cattle, the land of Transkei has been badly overgrazed, and this practice, together with primitive farming methods and periodically heavy rains, has resulted in serious soil erosion in many places. The potential of Transkei for tourism is clearly great, especially along its 150 miles of coastline, but as yet this potential has not been developed. Transkei's power resources are nonexistent, although hydroelectric development would seem a possibility, and such mineral deposits as there are exist in uncertain or uneconomic quantities. The most inexhaustible resource appears to be unskilled labor. Benbo reports that in recent years the Transkei labor force has grown annually by about 26,300 persons, but a generous estimate of the number of new jobs created in Transkei during the same period would be 7,000 annually.[11] Thus, nearly three-quarters of new job seekers have had to leave Transkei to find work, or remain unemployed. This point will be taken up again later.

● Nor is the physical infrastructure of Transkei impressive for an independent state. A single-track railway line winds its

10. Transkei Government, *Annual Report of the Transkei Public Service Commission, 1975*, p. 3.
11. *Transkei: Economic Review, 1975*, p. 31.

way between East London and Umtata, but Transkei depends on the South African Railways to maintain its rolling stock. Only the main road from East London to Natal is completely tarred. Transkei has but one port along its coast, Port St. Johns, at the mouth of the Mzimvubu River, but it has long been silted up and is incapable of handling ocean-going vessels without very substantial investment. Umtata and Butterworth have been declared economic growth points and each has grown appreciably in recent years. Umtata, in particular, has experienced a building boom associated with Transkei independence. But outside of these two centers the most evident characteristic of Transkei is its underdevelopment.

● The human resources of the territory are limited as well. Since the commencement of responsible government in 1964, about one-fifth of all Transkei expenses has been in the field of education. As a result, in 1972/73 no black country in the region had as high a proportion of its total population in school, and Transkei's expenditures on education per pupil were higher than in Botswana and more than twice the figure in Lesotho.[12] Nevertheless, at the time of the 1970 census it was found that 56.1 percent of the black population of Transkei had received no schooling at all, while those who went to school commonly stopped going after a few years. In 1974 less than 1 percent of all enrolled students were in the last two years of high school, whereas 63.9 percent were in the first four grades.[13] In August 1968 John d'Oliveira reported that more than 90 percent of Transkei teachers had themselves not graduated from high school.[14] A more serious fact is that the migratory labor system continually removes many of the most productive individuals from the territory, at least temporarily. Reflecting this exodus are statistics showing that women are twice as numerous as men in Transkei in the economically critical fifteen- to sixty-four-year-old age group.[15]

12. Benbo, *Black Development in South Africa* (Pretoria: Bureau for Economic Research Re Bantu Development, 1976), p. 202.
13. *Transkei: Economic Review, 1975,* pp. 56–57.
14. *The Star,* August 25, 1968.
15. Benbo, *Black Development,* p. 32.

A survey of half of Transkei's (current) twenty-eight
magisterial districts in January 1971 disclosed the existence
among a population of perhaps 1 million persons of just 43
black professionals.[16] And on the eve of independence, the
Financial Mail reported that in all of Transkei there were
only 135 doctors, and of these just 24 were black.[17] This
works out to 1 physician for every 14,333 resident Transkeians. The equivalent ratios in 1968 (shortly after the countries became independent) were 1:24,440 in Botswana,
1:31,670 in Lesotho, and 1:7,900 in Swaziland. The number
of professionals in Transkei ought to increase shortly, however. In 1974, 344 black Transkeians were enrolled in South
Africa's black universities.[18] Moreover, it seems probable
that the opportunities of living free from apartheid may draw
back to Transkei some educated Xhosa from the urban areas
of South Africa and even from overseas. Indeed, even before
independence there were several well-publicized examples of
the latter occurrence.

But without question Transkei's most serious affliction is
the poverty of its people. After a survey in 1968 of 2,185
households in the Bizana and Kentani districts of Transkei,
Johann Maree and P. J. de Vos estimated that 85.1 percent
of these households had incomes below the poverty datum
line, defined as the "theoretical absolute minimum requirements of a family to stay alive in the short run." The average
family income in these two districts among the families surveyed was in fact less than half this "absolute minimum."[19]
Not surprisingly, many fail to "stay alive." In 1973 Maree
reported estimates that in five Transkei districts as many as
40 percent of all African children die before the age of ten as
a direct or indirect result of malnutrition.[20]

16. Nancy C. J. Charton, "Black Elites in Transkei," *Politikon* 3,
no. 2 (October 1976): 71.
17. *Financial Mail (Special Report),* October 22, 1976, p. 15.
18. Benbo, *Black Development,* pp. 60, 203.
19. Johann Maree and P. J. de Vos, *Underemployment, Poverty and
Migrant Labour in the Transkei and Ciskei* (Johannesburg: S.A. Institute of Race Relations, 1975), pp. 2, 17, 21, 22.
20. Johann Maree, "Bantustan Economics," *Third World* 2, no. 6
(June 1973): 27.

• Although agriculture is the principal economic activity in Transkei, providing 35.2 percent of the territory's gross domestic product in 1973–74 and employing 78.5 percent of all economically active Xhosa in 1970[21], it is primarily small-scale subsistence farming (89 percent of the agricultural share of the GDP), which is notoriously inefficient. In an article that has been widely cited, Colin Bundy has argued that it was not always so. In the middle of the nineteenth century, Bundy writes, some African peasants, many of them in Transkei, competed successfully with whites for agricultural markets, and for a brief period, after the discovery of diamonds in Griqualand West in 1867 produced "a virtual explosion of peasant economic activity," Transkei knew material prosperity.[22] Yet by 1913 cattle epidemics, drought, the monopolistic practices of white traders, population pressures on the African lands, and the favored treatment accorded white farmers by government had impoverished this African peasantry and transformed many of its members into migrant laborers.

It is generally acknowledged that Transkei's well-watered interior plateau, comprising almost two-thirds of the territory, could be one of the best farming regions in the entire subcontinent. Benbo has referred to Transkei as the future "pantry" of South Africa.[23] Yet, in 1973–74, maize yields in Transkei (to take just one representative crop) were only 15 percent as large as the maize yields white farmers obtained in the Transvaal and the Orange Free State. And because livestock in Transkei are far more numerous than can be properly supported on the available pasturage, the quality of these animals is exceptionally poor. Government efforts to process and market meat in Transkei have lost money every year since they were begun in 1966.[24] In fact, the future "pantry" of South Africa has had to import most of its

21. *Transkei: Economic Review, 1975,* pp. 35, 38.

22. Colin Bundy, "The Emergence and Decline of a South African Peasantry," *African Affairs* 71, no. 285 (October 1972): 376.

23. *Transkei: Economic Review, 1975,* p. 43.

24. *Transkei In Dependence: Report of the Transkei Study Project* (Johannesburg: Wages and Economics Commission, SRC, University of the Witwatersrand, 1976), pp. 52, 53, 64.

annual food requirements from white South Africa, and the earnings of migrant workers have paid for them.[25]

The inefficient methods of peasant farming in Transkei arise primarily from two conditions: an agricultural labor force depleted by migrancy of many of its most productive persons, and plots too small to allow a surplus for reinvestment (for example, in better fertilizers) or the mechanization of agriculture. In 1955 an official blue-ribbon commission on the "socioeconomic development of the Bantu areas," the so-called Tomlinson Commission, recommended that the average African agricultural holding in Transkei be increased sharply to not less than fifty-seven acres, in order to return annually $138, considered an economic income for a family of six at 1955 prices. One-quarter of this land (fourteen acres) was to be arable. The commission believed that this plan would allow Transkei to support on the land about two-thirds of the persons then living there. The remainder would require new economic activities for their livelihood.[26] But in 1968 the study previously cited of the Bizana and Kentani districts showed that 95 percent of the families surveyed had holdings smaller than eleven acres of arable land, while the median family had just five arable acres.[27]

One consideration preventing the consolidation of land holdings in Transkei and thus perpetuating the inefficiency of peasant agriculture is the traditional system of land tenure. The principle underlying this system is that land is a communal and inalienable asset of the tribe, held in trust by the tribal chief and allocated by him among all married tribesmen. Every head of household is thus entitled to the use of a plot of arable land, and he also has the right to graze his livestock on a common pasture. But with a growing population, the land that a chief has to allocate to an individual household

25. *Financial Mail (Special Report),* October 22, 1976, p. 5.
26. Union of South Africa, *Summary of the Report of the Commission for the Socio-Economic Development of the Bantu Areas within the Union of South Africa.* U.G. 61/1955 (Pretoria: Government Printer, 1955), pp. 113, 115.
27. Maree and de Vos, *Underemployment, Poverty and Migrant Labour,* p. 13.

has been reduced to the point where it is uneconomic. The system prevents capitalization through land sales, and as grazing areas are held in common, there is no incentive for the individual farmer to cull his herd.[28] The Tomlinson Commission recommended in 1955 substitution of a system of freehold land tenure that would permit the creation of a full-time "Bantu farming class," and this idea has been echoed frequently since. But the proposal was rejected by Pretoria on the grounds that it would undermine the tribal structure in the African areas. There can be little doubt that the right to control the distribution of land is a primary source of the power of the chiefs in Transkei, and as ex-officio chiefs comprise half the membership of the new National Assembly, it is hard to imagine the government in Umtata adopting a different view in the near future. Moreover, it seems probable that privation of land ownership would be keenly resisted by many of those Transkei peasants for whom the traditional claim to at least some land may be their only protection against possible destitution.

● As noted earlier, it has been reliably estimated that the labor force in Transkei increases in size each year by approximately 26,300 persons. But in 1976 there were only about 50,000 paying jobs in all of the territory apart from subsistence agriculture.[29] This is not, in fact, unlike the situation in Lesotho, which, with a de facto population almost half as large as Transkei's, was estimated to have had just 21,000 persons in wage employment in 1973.[30] Obviously, as the figures for labor migration attest, neither of these countries can come near meeting the needs of their populations for work. Because of this, Transkei has been characterized as a "reservoir of cheap labour" for South African industry.[31] Without doubt Transkei performs this economic role and must continue to do so for the foreseeable future, and

28. *Transkei In Dependence*, p. 60.

29. *Financial Mail (Special Report)*, October 22, 1976, p. 12.

30. *Lesotho: A Development Challenge* (Washington, D.C.: The World Bank, 1975), p. 18.

31. Maree, "Bantustan Economics," p. 29.

Lesotho can scarcely be differentiated from Transkei in this respect.

Unpromising as this picture is now, it was worse a decade ago. Christopher Hill reports that in 1962 there were only 20,592 paying jobs in Transkei, over 8,000 of them in domestic service.[32] But because of an official policy that forbade the introduction of white capital into any African homeland, economic development of Transkei was then virtually at a standstill. The number of new jobs created in the territory each year was only several hundred at most, excluding the Transkei civil service that grew at the rate of about 200 new positions a year in the middle of the last decade. The establishment in 1965 of the Xhosa Development Corporation (XDC) with a mandate, in the words of its first chairman, "to plan and promote, in all spheres, the economic development of the Transkei and the African areas of the Ciskei"[33] did not immediately alter the situation, since the capital available to the XDC at first was just $1.15 million. In its fifth year the XDC had created only 3,416 new jobs in both Transkei and the Ciskei taken together.[34]

Then in 1968 the policy excluding white capital from Transkei was reversed.[35] To offset the absence of natural economic incentives that might encourage industry to locate in Transkei, Pretoria established a number of artificial incentives, known as "concessions." For example, an industrialist investing in Transkei can receive a 40 percent rebate on the cost of shipping his manufactured goods out of Transkei by railroad. And during the first several years of operations he is allowed

32. Christopher Hill, *Bantustans: The Fragmentation of South Africa* (London: Oxford University Press, 1964), p. 85.

33. *Transkei In Dependence*, p. 37.

34. Xhosa Development Corporation, *Ten Years of Progress: XDC in the Xhosa Homelands*, Tenth Annual Report, 1975, p. 57.

35. For a discussion of legislative policy regarding the development of the homelands, see Carter, Karis, and Stultz, *South Africa's Transkei*, chaps. 2 and 3. A more recent treatment will be found in Jeffrey Butler, Robert I. Rotberg, and John Adams, *The Black Homelands of South Africa: The Political and Economic Development of Bophuthatswana and KwaZulu* (Berkeley: University of California Press, 1977), chap. 3.

tax concessions on 10 percent of the value of manufacturing machinery and equipment and on 50 percent of the wages paid to African employees.[36] By the end of March 1974 such inducements had attracted seventeen enterprises to Transkei, all to either Butterworth or Umtata, the two growth centers. Excluding $7.5 million put up by the XDC (whose share capital had now risen to $46 million), this represented an investment in Transkei of $6 million of new private capital. In this way, 2,362 new jobs were created, at an average cost somewhat under the $6,900 that has been set as the average investment required to create one new industrial job in the so-called decentralized areas of South Africa.[37]

In passing it should be pointed out that it has been estimated that a job in agriculture would have cost only one-sixth as much as a job in industry, and recognition of this fact has caused Merle Lipton to question the goal of non-agricultural employment for Transkei, which has been the premise of most thinking about the territory's development from whatever quarter. "Given these endowments of land and labour—and the scarcity of capital—the obvious strategy," she writes, "is to go for a labour intensive agriculture."[38] Indeed, the Transkei government itself has undertaken some commercial crop production (for example, of tea, Phormium tenax, and timber) in which perhaps 9,000 persons are now employed. But the agricultural interests of the XDC (which became the Transkei Development Corporation, TDC, on August 1, 1976) have been relatively few. In fact, though Lipton's proposal has received respectful consideration, expert opinion is skeptical that labor-intensive agriculture can provide the solution to Transkei's, or any homeland's, employment problem. Two militating factors are cited: the great amount of time that would be required to refashion a

36. Transkei Development Corporation, *Information for Potential Investors in the Transkei* Umtata, April 1976, p. 3.

37. *Transkei: Economic Review, 1975*, p. 48; *Transkei In Dependence*, p. 42.

38. Merle Lipton, "The South African Census and the Bantustan Policy," *World Today* 28, no. 6 (June 1972): 264.

peasant agriculture based on a different tradition, and the extent of soil erosion in the homelands.[39]

Shortly before Transkei independence the rate of job creation in the territory accelerated. A table depicting the number of jobs created for Africans by all of the activities of the XDC during the first decade of the corporation's existence showed that 22 percent of these positions appeared in the last year.[40] And in just one year, 1975, the size of the Transkei civil service (excluding teachers) increased by 89 percent, to stand at 11,554 posts in early 1976. In the next twelve months it increased again by half, to 17,320 positions at the end of the year.[41] Obviously this development was directly related to preparations for independence, and future growth in the number of civil service positions should be much more gradual. Nevertheless, in 1975, under the most favorable conditions, it seems likely that fewer than 10,350 new paying jobs were created in Transkei, or only about 40 percent of those needed to accommodate the estimated number of new job seekers in that year.

• In view of the described adverse economic conditions of Transkei, it is no surprise to find that the per capita income of the territory in 1971 was about $69. This is certainly desperately low, but it is actually higher than the equivalent figure for Lesotho and Burundi (calculated for 1970) and just under the figure for Somalia. But when one takes the earnings of Transkei's migrant workers into account (which constituted 69.6 percent of Transkei's gross national income in 1973), the per capita income for Transkei (1973 figures) jumps to $201 annually. On this basis, Transkei must be placed just above the median of twenty-one African countries surveyed with respect to GNI per capita.[42] Because of its economic relations with the republic, therefore, Transkei obtains some relief from circumstances that would other-

39. Gavin Maasdorp, *Economic Development Strategy in the African Homelands: The Role of Agriculture and Industry* (Johannesburg: S.A. Institute of Race Relations, May 1974), p. 14.

40. XDC, *Ten Years of Progress*, p. 57.

41. Republic of Transkei, *Annual Report of the Public Service Commission, 1976*, p. 3.

42. Benbo, *Black Development*, p. 201.

wise place it among Africa's (and the world's) poorest states—nearly destitute, but not uniquely so. With these relations, however, Transkei, though still poor, gains parity—economically speaking—with a great many African states.

• According to figures compiled by Benbo, the per capita expenditure of the Transkei government in 1973-74 was $42.55.[43] This is three times the level of Lesotho or Malawi during the same period and puts Transkei in the upper third of twenty-one African countries surveyed by Benbo. But as a result of this comparatively high level of government expenditure, Transkei has for years been unable to finance its current (that is, noncapital) budget alone. Theo Malan, an economist at the Africa Institute in Pretoria, has estimated that about 80 percent of Transkei's 1976-77 budget of $156 million was earmarked for current expenditures.[44] Yet, since the beginning of the present budgeting arrangements in 1964, Transkei's domestic sources have never accounted for more than 24.2 percent of yearly Transkei revenues. Apart from surpluses carried over, the balance each year has been subscribed by the republic, varying from 61.9 percent of total income in 1965-66 to a high of 77.4 percent in 1974-75. In 1976-77 the republic's contribution was $107 million. Some of this yearly grant from the republic represented customs and excise duties collected by the South African government on goods destined for Transkei, and after independence similar remittances are expected to continue as Transkei is extended membership, de facto if not de jure, in the regional customs union for which Pretoria is the administering (that is, collecting) partner. The annual grant also reflected taxes paid to the republic by Transkei citizens, and under the terms of the Financial Arrangements with the Transkei Act, 1976, Pretoria has agreed to continue indefinitely transferring such monies to Umtata, and not to regard them as income due to the republic. On the basis of these agreements, it has been asserted that the new state will probably be able to meet its current expenditures each year out of its own resources, to-

43. Ibid., p. 203.
44. Theo Malan, "Transkei—Economically Viable?" *Africa Institute Bulletin* 14, nos. 7 and 8 (1976): 254.

gether with that external income to which it is now legally (that is, by treaty) entitled.[45] It has thus been concluded that Transkei will be dependent on foreign aid only for its capital funding.

Even in its own terms, I find this prediction overly optimistic. In 1973-74, for example, at the height of a period of mineral development requiring extraordinary imports, Botswana (whose GDP has been substantially larger than Transkei's) earned just $24 million through its membership in the regional customs union.[46] Yet the difference in 1976-77 between 80 percent of Transkei's budget and the total of revenues expected from within the territory was $75.7 million. But the categories themselves are suspect. The agreement of South Africa to remit to Umtata the taxes paid by Transkei citizens in the republic is in fact a form of disguised foreign aid. After all, taxes paid by Americans or European nationals in the republic are not remitted to their governments. Moreover, only a small minority of the Transkei "citizens" in question, namely, the migrant workers, are, as we have said previously, ever likely to return to Transkei or to be in a position to profit from the activities of the Transkei government. It thus seems more truthful to say that in 1976-77 Transkei was dependent on a gift of approximately $40 million from South Africa, or about one-third of the funds required, to meet just its current expenditures. In fact, this position was considerably better than in neighboring Lesotho during the early years of its independence, when, according to Weisfelder, Great Britain made up the difference between territorial revenues and recurrent expenditures that were about 2.5 times larger.[47]

Having defined "Transkei's share," I now have three questions. First, does this division of the common South African

---

45. Ibid.; Matanzima, *Address to the Nation*, p. 6.

46. *Africa South of the Sahara, 1974* (London: Europa Publications, 1974), pp. 166, 169.

47. Richard F. Weisfelder, "Lesotho," in Christian P. Potholm and Richard Dale, eds., *Southern Africa in Perspective: Essays in Regional Politics* (New York: The Free Press, 1972), pp. 133-34.

estate constitute the beginning (in the words of D. V. Cowen) of a "fair partition" of the country? I refer specifically to partition rather than federation because on its face that is the goal of the policy we are examining. Second, is Transkei credible as a sovereign nation-state from the standpoint of its material and human endowments? And finally, can Transkei realistically be expected to act independently of South Africa?

Some will argue that only the first of these questions really matters, because if the division of the resources of South Africa that is entailed in Transkei independence is basically unfair and one-sided from the standpoint of the black man, it should be vigorously opposed, for it cannot in the end bring lasting peace to the region because African grievances will remain. It makes no difference in this circumstance whether or not Transkei is truly independent of Pretoria, or whether it can perhaps be compared with some other independent states in various parts of the world. Put baldly, this is the view that the right of Transkeians to choose independence on the basis of an unfair division of resources should not be recognized because such a choice brings "incalculable harm to the African majority within South Africa by segmenting it" and undermining its claims for equality.[48] Here I am operating on the basis of a different and simpler notion, that is, that Transkeians ought to be accorded the right to choose independence if, on objective grounds, Transkei can be compared with other states whose sovereign existence is widely recognized. In short, I am unwilling to arrogate to myself (especially in the name of democracy) the right to determine the appropriate political destiny for 2.3 million Transkeians living in the territory, or to deny them the right to do so if their concrete situation is indistinguishable from that of other peoples whose own right to self-determination has not been previously disputed. Obviously, from this point of view, the practical circumstances of Lesotho are particulary interesting because the political predicament of its people vis-à-vis the

48. Gwendolen M. Carter, *American Policy and the Search for Justice and Reconciliation in South Africa* (Racine, Wisconsin: The Johnson Foundation, 1976), p. 39.

republic before 1966 would seem to have been much the same as Transkei's, perhaps even less desperate. For unlike Transkei, Lesotho had an option between sovereign independence and incorporation into the republic, namely, remaining as a British colony indefinitely. There are of course other aspects to this issue of the "right to choose independence," specifically, whether the choice given the Transkei electorate was a free one, or whether their actual decision was not made under duress, that is, the threat of their perpetual subordination to apartheid. This question will be discussed further in chapter 3.

Does Transkei independence signify commencement of a fair partition of South Africa along racial lines? Consideration of the intriguing question of what "fairness" ought to mean in such a context, and how we might recognize a "fair partition" were it to occur, will be discussed in chapter 6. It seems possible to delay dealing with these issues now because, on its face, the division of the resources of South Africa discussed here falls far short of the requirements of a fair partition by *any* reasonable definition of these terms. Africa's richest country, with an annual per capita income for all its citizens of over $600, has sired one of Africa's three or four poorest and weakest countries. Transkei has inherited little in the way of industry or infrastructure, and, except for farmland, it has almost nothing in the way of natural resources. Its people are deeply impoverished and in many cases have no work. It is no exaggeration to say that all of the modern, urban, and industrialized civilization of South Africa has been withheld from the new state. The conclusion scarcely needs belaboring, for the evidence is overwhelming. Materially speaking, Transkei independence represents a highly one-sided separation.

Does Transkei then lack credibility as a sovereign nation-state? But what should "credibility" mean in this context? Similarity to other existing states? In terms of the level of its development and its natural resources, Transkei is, excluding the assistance of South Africa, similar to a few (but just a few) of the poorest countries of the world. It would, however, appear to be marginally more developed and more promising than its immediate northern neighbor, Lesotho. In the aggregate, it would seem that the "life chances" of Transkeians (again excluding South African help) are probably equivalent to the least affluent 10 to 20 percent of the national populations of the so-called Third World. And with South African assistance, Transkeians, poor as they still are, are probably not worse off than a much higher percentage of the citizens of the Third World.

Perhaps national "credibility" should mean that a state meets certain abstract standards. This appeared to be the sense of a report appearing in the Johannesburg *Star* on September 29, 1976. The report stated that Great Britain had decided not to recognize Transkei (in the words of the British announcement) "on the occasion of its purported independence." The paper quoted the British foreign secretary as explaining, "It is clear the Transkei will not fulfill our well-established legal criteria for recognition as an independent state." The report gave no indication what these criteria might be, but the suggestion that in deciding whether or not to recognize a state the British government (or indeed any government) regularly and consistently applies some set of objective standards to that state must be rejected as empirically false and perhaps self-serving. In fact, sovereign states recognize other states when they deem it in their individual self-interest to do so. No one can doubt that many countries would eagerly extend diplomatic recognition to Umtata were Transkei found to have a monopoly over the supply of some critical commodity. Only when such self-interest is weak or unclear can a state afford to rely on abstract standards. When this *is* the case, it has been observed that three standards are usually applied: Does the state under consideration have established boundaries? Does it have a settled population? And does it have a government that is in effective control of its territory?[49] If we ignore (as ultimately we cannot) the

49. G. N. Barrie, "A legal view of Transkei recognition and so-called 'Statelessness,' " *Politikon* 3, no. 2 (October 1976): 31–32; Robert Schrire, "The Emancipation of Transkei," *The World Today* 33, no. 1 (January 1977): 36.

complicating factor of the urban Xhosa, who are (in the view of some) Transkei citizens, it may be thought that Transkei meets these standards and is thus credible.

Many, however, have felt it necessary to apply a more demanding standard to Transkei. For these individuals Transkei ought to have a viable economy in order to be regarded credible as a sovereign state. The idea of course is that a state lacking economic viability would be too weak to be independent, whatever its formal legal position. The concept of economic viability has been variously interpreted, but two principles are common.[50] One is that an economically viable state should be able to provide employment for a substantial majority of its citizens. Here, as we have seen, Transkei falls short. The territory itself can provide work for only about 58 percent of its domestic work force, ignoring those persons settled permanently outside Transkei. At any time, 50 percent of Transkei males between the ages of fifteen and sixty-five years are away in South Africa.[51] The equivalent figure for Lesotho is about 60 percent.[52] Nor is there any reason to believe that this situation can be improved soon.

The second principle is that an economically viable state ought to be able to finance its current (noncapital) expenditures out of its own resources. But this Transkei has never been able to do, as has been seen. In the case of Lesotho, British grants-in-aid financed more than half of the country's current budget up to 1968–69. But thereafter, the government held the level of services constant in real terms in order to reduce Lesotho's dependence on Great Britain, and these grants were stopped altogether in 1974.[53] As Transkei's levels of official services at the point of independence were comparatively high by Third World standards, such a strategy might have recommended itself to Umtata in order to lessen Transkei's dependence on the republic. But when the 1977–78 "estimates" appeared in March 1977, it became clear that no

50. Malan, "Transkei—Economically Viable?" p. 253.

51. Deduction from Table 5.1.5, *Transkei: Economic Revue, 1975*, p. 32.

52. *Lesotho: A Development Challenge*, p. 18.

53. Ibid., p. xvii.

such strategy had been adopted, for the provisional 1977-78 budget showed an increase from the preceding year of 75 percent, only a small part of which could be accounted for by inflation. And the share of total revenues expected to be provided by Transkei's own sources, even with striking increases in local taxation, fell to just 15.9 percent, lower than the year before. The contribution expected from the republic in 1977-78 was $190 million (including Transkei's share of customs receipts), up from $107 million in 1976-77. These funds do not include the share capital of the Transkei Development Corporation, all of which is subscribed by Pretoria.

But what has put a curse on Transkei independence, at least in part, is not just that the territory lacks economic viability. There are, after all, a good many states that are not economically viable, although among them Transkei is probably less viable than most. The principal difficulty is Transkei's exclusive and seemingly willing economic reliance on just one state, and that state South Africa, whose good will toward African aspirations is suspect in the world-at-large. It is a problem for Transkei because of South Africa's low prestige in current world affairs and because it would seem inevitably to compromise seriously Umtata's freedom to adopt policies at odds with strongly held views of Pretoria. This is of course a strict standard of political independence that some other of the world's ministates might have difficulty meeting. Moreover, it suggests, unreasonably, I believe, that the principal value of national self-determination for a people is the gratification they gain from taking a step a powerful neighbor emphatically opposes. Clearly, the Transkei state is not able to do this. But certainly independence also means, and most of the time for most states, the ability merely to manage one's own mundane affairs freely, in which matters one's neighbors usually have no interest at all. The Transkei state is doubtless not free to damage the interests of South Africa, but its economic and financial dependence on Pretoria would not appear to restrict its freedom to do most of the things states do—for example, collect taxes, make laws, allocate scarce resources, and educate and police its population.

3

WHO CHOSE INDEPENDENCE?

This chapter takes up certain distinctively political issues.
However, there will be no effort to produce a general history
of recent Transkei politics. That has already been ably done,
at least to the middle of 1976, by Patrick Laurence in his previously cited work. Instead, an attempt will be made to
match the reality of the political decision-making that moved
Transkei to independence against the political requirements
of separatism, as discussed in chapter 1.

Reviewing that discussion, we find that most of the authors covered spent less time dealing with the politics of partition, or of federating, than considering economic and material implications. The reason for this, I take it, is not that the
political dimension of the process of separating conflicting parties is unimportant or easy, but rather that the political needs
of the situation are simply stated: the willing consent of all
participating groups. All our writers would appear to agree
with Tiryakian that a partition (or other) arrangement that
leaves a substantial body of the overall population feeling that
they have been cheated, or that they are still subordinate to
their former adversaries, is not likely to be successful.

Indeed, it seems arguable that the requirement of general
consent should be seen as a stricter requirement in the case of

southern Africa, if separatism in some form is to succeed, than it has been in other parts of the world where separatist solutions to desperate conflicts have been effective. The reason for this is that no contemporary proponent of separatism in southern Africa contemplates a complete, or total, physical separatism of black and white as R. F. A. Hoernlé did in 1939. Today it is accepted that even if an idealized form of separatism should come to pass, millions of Africans (to say nothing of coloureds and Asians) would still be found among the whites on a daily basis. Lacking substantial African consent, then, white South Africa might, in the manner of (pre-June 1967) Israel, have not only to protect its borders against hostile neighbors but also, unlike Israel, concurrently to deal with a sizable alienated population in its midst. Taking into account the state power relationships in the region, it seems possible to imagine that with its domestic flank secure, white South Africa might be able to survive, indeed even to prosper, although surrounded on all sides by enemies. But with its domestic scene also vulnerable to widespread civil strife and work stoppages, there are few commentators who are prepared to grant white South Africans a secure future. African consent for Transkei independence is thus a key issue, indeed perhaps *the* key issue.

Transkei elections

In a recent article, Roger J. Southall, who from his base in Lesotho is among the best-informed and insightful of the new writers on Transkei, concluded as follows concerning the issue of African consent:

> The indications are that in the case of Transkei, the majority of Homeland citizens either have strongly opposed independence (which would legally deprive them of their claim to share in the wealth and future of South Africa as a whole), or have been pressurised [*sic*] to accept their changed status.[1]

1. Roger J. Southall, "The Beneficiaries of Transkeian 'Independence'," *Journal of Modern African Studies* 15, no. 1 (1977): 4.

On its face, this is a surprising statement, for less than a month before independence, on September 29, Transkei held its fourth general election. The results were a one-sided victory for the ruling Transkei National Independence party (TNIP), which, as its name suggests, ran on the issue of Transkei independence. TNIP won 71 of 75 elected seats in the new parliament. And three years before this, in 1973, TNIP won 25 of 45 elective seats in the Transkei Legislative Assembly and 55.2 percent of the popular vote in an election preceding which Matanzima mentioned the possibility of independence for Transkei within five years.[2] Southall is of course fully aware of these results, but he dismisses them as a distortion of public opinion in Transkei. He grounds this view on several specified objections to the Transkei electoral system.

One objection concerns the so-called urban vote. The 1963 Transkei Constitution established a universal adult franchise for all Transkei citizens, and this principle was carried over in the 1976 constitution, section 24, although under a somewhat broader definition of citizenship. But it will be remembered that approximately one-third of all Transkei citizens now live permanently outside Transkei, most in urban areas of the republic. Electorally, these "non-resident" citizens have been treated as absentee voters. They have been eligible, indeed encouraged, to vote in each of the four Transkei general elections that have been held since 1963. In the election of 1973, for example, 330 polling stations for Transkei voters were established in the "white" areas, and the length of the polling period was extended for these voters to fifteen days.[3] However, when cast, the votes of such individuals have been counted in the total of votes cast in their respective "home" constituencies in Transkei. There are no constituencies represented in the Transkei legislature that are outside the borders of Transkei, although on May 26, 1972, the Transkei Legislative Assembly unanimously moved that the republican govern-

2. H. J. Kotze, "The Transkei General Election," *Africa Institute Bulletin* 6, no. 9 (1973): 352.
3. Ibid., p. 351.

ment should be asked to agree to the establishment of five such seats.[4]

The foremost argument cited in the TLA in favor of this proposal was that it would remove from elected members the burden of traveling to many distant areas of the republic in order to maintain contact with their constituents. Pretoria rejected this suggestion, however, on the grounds that it would establish electoral divisions outside the Transkei government's area of jurisdiction.[5] Southall appears to find in this a deliberate effort to reduce the influence of the urban vote on Transkei politics, and it is clear that the existing arrangement does effectively "gerrymander" the total urban vote and the vote in individual urban centers, spreading it across all of Transkei's electoral districts (currently twenty-eight). Yet it is hard to see how any arrangement that would not have this effect could be consistent with the idea of political separate development. In fact, the electoral arrangements governing the Transkei urban vote are similar to the arrangements that apply to United States citizens who live outside of the United States. The important difference, of course, is that these citizens are a tiny percentage of the entire American electorate, whereas if all Transkeians outside Transkei who are eligible for the franchise did in fact register and vote, they might represent as much as 43 percent of the entire Transkei electorate.

In fact, as Southall also points out, electoral participation on the part of eligible persons has been far greater within Transkei than outside it, and this difference appears to have increased since the first election in 1963. At that time I estimated that 97 percent of eligible persons within Transkei did register, as compared to 50 percent of those in the cities. And on election day 77.1 percent of registered persons actually voted in Transkei, against a figure of 51.7 percent outside. A

4. Republic of South Africa, Transkei Government, *Debates of the Transkei Legislative Assembly, Fifth Session, Second Assembly, 12 April 1972 – 13 June 1972.* (Umtata: Elata Commercial Printers, 1972), p. 337.

5. *A Survey of Race Relations in South Africa, 1973* (Johannesburg: S.A. Institute of Race Relations, 1974), p. 158.

decade later, extrapolating from figures supplied H. J. Kotze,[6] the likelihood of a Transkei citizen being a registered voter was nearly three times as great within the territory as elsewhere. Moreover, on election day only 12 percent of the vote was cast outside Transkei, down from 20 percent in 1963, and this low level of participation on the part of urban voters is thought to have continued in 1976.[7] The number of candidates in each of the four elections from outside Transkei shows the same pattern: 8 of 180 in 1963, 11 of 146 in 1968, 0 of 96 in 1973, and 0 of 161 in 1976.[8]

There are doubtless structural factors contributing to this low level of electoral participation in the cities. Hennie Kotze has written, for example, that in 1976, opposition parties did not visit voters in the Witwatersrand and Cape Town because of a shortage of funds.[9] But many writers have suggested a deeper reason, namely, a positive desire on the part of most urban Africans to be dissociated from homeland affairs.[10] What seems clear is that Transkei citizens living permanently outside Transkei have not consented to their permanent exclusion from the rights of citizenship in so-called white South Africa. From the perspective of Transkei, this fact may not be important if, as I and Matanzima assume, these individuals never return, that is, if they continue to live in South Africa. For South Africa, however, this situation means the continuation of the critical alienation of a substantial number of its resident population. And obviously it signifies the continuation of a high potential for civil strife that such alienation supports, primarily in the cities of the republic.

Southall's second point is that Transkei elections have been conducted unfairly in order to encumber individuals

6. H. J. Kotze, "The Transkei General Election," p. 351.
7. Hennie Kotze, "The Transkei General Election," *Africa Institute Bulletin* 14, nos. 9 and 10 (1976): 342.
8. Ibid., p. 340; Patrick Laurence, *The Transkei: South Africa's Politics of Partition* (Johannesburg: Ravan Press, 1976), p. 86.
9. Hennie Kotze, "The Transkei General Election," p. 341.
10. Philip Mayer, *Urban Africans and the Bantustans* (Johannesburg: S.A.Institute of Race Relations, 1972), p. 19; Melville Leonard Edelstein, *What Do Young Africans Think?* (Johannesburg: Labour and Community Consultants, 1974), p. 96; Laurence, *The Transkei*, p. 86.

opposed to the policy of separate development. Here there are two issues. The lesser one emerges from the fact that Transkei ballot papers allow no symbols to designate either parties or candidates. In consequence, illiterate voters (and many voters in Transkei are illiterate) must declare them-selves verbally before official poll watchers. A government circular states, "If you do not know how to vote you may ask the presiding officer to vote for you in the presence of two witnesses." Such witnesses are often local headmen, lesser officials of the administration, who are usually per-sonally familiar with the individual voters in their areas. Under such circumstances it is not surprising that many votes are neither secret nor free.

Most observers feel that the tribesmen of Transkei would tend to vote the wishes of their chiefs and headmen in any event and, therefore, the net impact of this situation in terms of election results is probably not great. Moreover, these regulations have existed from the time of the first election in 1963, which most observers were prepared to accept as a free and democratic expression of public sentiment in Transkei. Indeed, the widespread defeat in 1963 of candidates favor-able to the present prime minister has often been cited since as the proof that the people of Transkei reject separate development.

The second issue is more weighty and makes it possible for persons who accept the 1963 results as valid to reject the 1976 results, which this time were overwhelmingly favorable to the Matanzima government. This is the application of the extraordinary security powers of the state to stifle political opposition. The primary instrument is known as Proclama-tion R400 which was promulgated in Transkei in November 1960 to help contain a peasant rebellion against the so-called Bantu Authorities system in Eastern Pondoland and kept in force thereafter. Proclamation R400 gives the police the right to detain persons without trial and extends a number of arbi-trary powers to the chiefs.[11] Yet several close followers of Transkei doubt that the collapse of the several opposition

11. For details, see *A Survey of Race Relations, 1961,* pp. 43–47.

parties that have existed in the territory since 1963 owes much to the use, or threat of use, of Proclamation R400, at least until recently; although this is not to suggest that it has not been applied. In 1974, for example, it is reported that a total of nineteen Africans were arrested in Transkei under Proclamation R400 and detained for varying periods.[12] Shortly before the 1976 general election, however, the leader of the (newly radical) Democratic party, Hector Ncokasi, was detained, and shortly nearly every member of his executive staff was arrested as well, including a number of actual or potential candidates. At independence, on October 26, all were still in jail. Clearly these detentions may have affected the outcome of the election regarding a number of seats. Yet, as the Democratic party (one of two opposition parties in 1976) seemed ready to contest fewer than one-fourth of all seats, it can scarcely be maintained that had these detentions not occurred, TNIP would have lost the 1976 election or that a position hostile to independence might have prevailed. Practically speaking, as we shall see, Transkei's course toward independence had been set irreversibly months, even years before. Still, it is hard to imagine how greater damage could have been done to the prestige of the new state, or, indirectly, to the credibility of separate development, than was effected by these detentions when they occurred.

The power of the chiefs
The third point concerns the legislative power of chiefs in the Transkei parliament and is perhaps the strongest reason for believing that popular opinion may have been distorted in the policy-making process. Transkei is, of course, not unique in Africa in having ex-officio chiefs in its legislature. W. J. Breytenbach has noted that this has been the case in the national, unicameral, parliaments of both Gambia and Sierra Leone.[13] However, no other African country approaches the

12. Republic of South Africa, *House of Assembly Debates,* February 11, 1975, col. 96.
13. W. J. Breytenbach, "Chieftainship and Political Development in the Homelands," *Africa Institute Bulletin* 13, nos. 9 and 10 (1975): 329.

proportion of chiefs in its lower house that is found in Transkei. (At the time of independence, Lesotho and Botswana had upper houses composed entirely of chiefs or the representatives of chiefs.) In 1975, for example, the Sierra Leone House of Representatives consisted of 100 members, 12 of whom were paramount chiefs. But when the Transkei Legislative Assembly was established in 1963, 64 of its 109 members (58 percent) were chiefs sitting ex officio, and in the new National Assembly, as pointed out above, elected and ex-officio members are equally balanced in a house of 150.

Hammond-Tooke has written that in traditional Cape Nguni culture, the tribal chief "was never a despot."[14] He could not generally "go against the wishes of his people; he could never move faster than the pace of the majority of his tribesmen." Accordingly, traditional political authority in Transkei was consensual. From the time of the territory's annexation until 1956, the substantial removal of chiefs from the structure of direct rule under which Transkei was administered allowed the chiefs to maintain much of their traditional prestige and popularity, for in this bureaucratic system the centrally appointed location headmen "assumed the scapegoat role".[15] However, in 1956 the system of direct rule in Transkei was superseded by the Bantu Authorities system which, working through a hierarchy of tribal, regional, and territorial councils, sought to reassert and strengthen the powers of the chiefs. The result was to place the chiefs in Transkei in an "intercalary" position, as Hammond-Tooke has described in his book *Command or Consensus: The Development of Transkeian Local Government.* Not only were the chiefs responsible for carrying out the wishes of their people, they were at the same time obliged to act as loyal representatives of the white bureaucracy. Inevitably, this produced an insoluble dilemma that undermined the prestige of the chiefs by periodically pitting them against their own tribesmen.

14. W. D. Hammond-Tooke, *Command or Consensus: The Development of Transkeian Local Government* (Cape Town: David Philip, 1975), pp. 211–12.
15. Ibid., p. 103.

An example of this occurred very early in the life of the TLA and illustrated the importance of the chiefs in the legislative process. In December 1963 Chief Kaiser Matanzima defeated Paramount Chief Victor Poto in the election of the first chief minister of Transkei, even though he was supported by only 12 of the 45 elected members of the TLA. This was possible because 42 chiefs voted for Matanzima and only 16 for Poto. The issue was thus decided by the chiefs, who overturned the clear verdict of the first Transkei general election, held just a month before, on November 20. For though political parties were not yet formally in existence in Transkei, the 1963 election was fought by most candidates as a contest between Poto and the doctrine of "multiracialism" and the unity of South Africa on the one hand and Matanzima and separate development on the other.[16] At the time it was assumed by most observers that the chiefs had capitulated to pressures from Pretoria. As salaried adminstrators in the structure of Transkei administration, whose removal from office is not unknown, it seemed plausible that the chiefs would be particularly sensitive to Pretoria's wishes.

However, five years later, after the 1968 general election, the Matanzima government was supported by a majority of the elected members (28 of 45) as well as by a majority of the chiefs (56 of 64), and this support among the elected members continued to grow until 1976 when Matanzima enjoyed virtually equivalent (and overwhelming) strength among both groups of parliamentarians. (See table.) Thus, should the ex-officio chiefs now be removed entirely from the Transkei National Assembly, Prime Minister Matanzima would not lose power, although as an ex-officio member himself, he would need to secure election. In a formal sense, the distortion of popular opinion on the floor of the TLA that did exist after 1963 because of the participation of the chiefs was remedied after the second election, and since then the presence of chiefs in the legislature may be said merely to have amplified popular majorities rather than to have overturned them.

16. Carter, Karis, and Stultz, *South Africa's Transkei,* chap. 7.

Comparison of Transkei General Elections, 1963–1976

Year	1963	1968	1973	1976
Registered voters	880,425	907,778	952,369	1,083,175
Votes cast	601,204	451,916	323,092	354,489
Percentage poll (adjusted)	68.3%	52.6%	42.3%	43.5%
Candidates	180	146	96	161
Unopposed candidates	0	3	5	16
Results:*				
TNIP	15	28	27	71
Democratic party	29	14	10	1
New Democratic party				2
Independents	1	3	8	1
Gov't majority thereafter	33	59	63	136

*Parties were not formed until after the 1963 election. Results for 1963 are as of the establishment of parties early in 1964.

The issue of the chiefs in the Transkei legislature cannot be dismissed so easily, however. Government spokesmen have often referred to the chiefs as the "natural leaders" of Transkei, but in its legislative sense this point is not supported by the foremost authority on the anthropology of the area. Of the chief among the Cape Nguni, Hammond-Tooke has written, "He was always a conservative element, the interpreter and upholder of tradition, seldom a legislator. He was only in rare, and sometimes spectacular, instances an initiator of social change."[17] Thus, there can be no doubt that the presence of so many chiefs in parliament biases the decisions of that institution in a conservative and progovernment direction. In view of this, it seems probable that one reason why no opposition group has succeeded in Transkei since 1963 is the widespread recognition, confirmed in the first election, that with most of the chiefs likely to support the regime, even a very strong showing in an election might not be sufficient to remove TNIP from office. The chiefs in the TLA, and now the National Assembly, are the prime minister's "reserve troops"; he has not needed them to prevail in the legis-

17. Hammond-Tooke, *Command or Consensus,* p. 212.

lature for nearly a decade, but none of his political opponents can have failed to take them into account.

Southall cites two other behavioral factors (that is, not related to the system itself) he feels also cast doubt on the contention that Transkei election results truly reflect popular opinion in Transkei. One of these is that opposition parties, for whatever reasons, have not always contested all or even most constituencies, with the result that some persons who may have been opposed to the Matanzima regime had no opposition candidate to vote for. In 1968, 3 of 45 members were returned unopposed, and in 1973 the figure was 5. But in 1976 Transkei took a major step toward becoming a de facto one-party state. Opposition candidates were entered in only ten of all twenty-eight constituencies, contesting a total of just 26 of 75 seats. In six constituencies electing 16 members, TNIP candidates were returned unopposed; no votes were cast here at all. And in twelve constituencies returning 33 members, all 86 candidates supported TNIP. Conceivably in these seats every vote should be counted "for independence." Obviously, the results of an election with this kind of structure are an uncertain guide to what the true attitudes of the voters are on a specific policy issue, in this instance Transkei independence.

The second point concerns voter turnout in Transkei elections. In 1963 the percentage poll was 68.3 percent. Five years later it fell to 52.6 percent, adjusted for uncontested seats, and in 1973 it fell again to 42.3 percent, similarly adjusted. In 1976 the poll in contested constituencies was 43.5 percent. Southall is not alone in suggesting that declining voter participation after 1963 signifies a progressive alienation of the Transkei electorate from homeland politics and that this offsets the steady rise in TNIP's share of the total vote—from 44 percent in 1968 to 55.2 percent in 1973. (The 1976 figure is unknown but obviously is higher still.) The implication is that the Matanzima government has remained since 1963 a minority government from the standpoint of its absolute popular support. Writing before the 1976 vote, the authors of *Transkei In Dependence* stated, "Taking all eligible voters into account it seems that Matanzima is accepting 'independence' for the Transkei with the support of less than 15% of the people."[18]

In a sense this claim is unfair. Few democratic governments have been supported by a majority of all theoretically eligible or even registered voters, at least in countries where registration and voting are voluntary. Nonetheless, a 43.5 percent voter turnout one month before independence would seem low. If, however, we exclude the so-called urban Xhosa from these calculations—their interest in Transkei affairs, as seen above, is widely conceded to be small—the overall percentage poll *within* Transkei in 1976 rises to the range of 50 to 55 percent. Viewed in the light of the one-sided nature of the 1976 election and its predictable outcome in terms of party strengths in the new National Assembly, such an average turnout within Transkei may not be particularly surprising or politically significant.

Taken together, all of these factors—the "gerrymandered" urban vote, Proclamation R400, the role of the chiefs, the large number of uncontested seats in 1976, and the low levels of voter turnout (especially in the cities)—give credence to Southall's charge that despite his unassailable parliamentary position, Matanzima "had little claim to a popular mandate for leading the Transkei to independence."[19] It is a difficult question, in part because the concept of an electoral "mandate" is vague, but I believe that Southall is correct. He has not demonstrated his more sweeping contention that a majority of Transkei citizens either "strongly opposed" Transkei independence or were "pressurised" (presumably against their wishes) to accept it. In regard to the suggestion of coercion, Southall's most telling evidence, the 1976 detentions of the executive of the small Democratic party (in the last TLA just two members belonged to the DP), could not have had such a general effect. Certainly since 1968 there has been no mandate not to seek independence, that is, to keep Transkei a part of South Africa, which was Chief Poto's position in 1963. But the equation of TNIP's strength in parliament with public support for independence *is* unconvincing for all of

18. *Transkei In Dependence,* p. 6.
19. Southall, "Beneficiaries," p. 8.

the reasons Southall cites. What is clear is the fact that because the meaningfulness of Transkei election results can be questioned by fair-minded persons, the political separation of Transkei from South Africa lacks that critical and widely accepted legitimacy a more democratic decision-making process might have provided.

The issue here is not primarily the democratic nature of the structure of government in Transkei (the world appears to have a high tolerance for undemocratic regimes, especially in Africa), but whether or not the specific decision to separate Transkei from the rest of South Africa represented the true wishes of the Transkei people. If it did not, the contribution of Transkei independence to reducing tensions in the region would appear problematical. Indeed, one could argue that even if it did represent popular sentiment in Transkei, that would not necessarily signify that Transkeian blacks have renounced their previous claims for equal participation in a common South African society (though in a public relations sense it would be a considerable moral victory for the whites). For in deciding on the issue of independence, the choice presented to Transkeians (to the extent that they had a choice) was not between Transkei independence and participation in a democratic and nonracial South Africa. The alternative was, rather, the racial status quo in southern Africa. It is conceivable that some Africans may have concluded that Transkei independence was preferable to the status quo for the foreseeable future without necessarily abandoning a longer term aspiration to share in the new opportunities of a wholly "liberated" subcontinent. But obviously if the people of Transkei should feel that independence was forced on them by Pretoria in opposition to their own wishes and to further the selfish interests of whites, the result, at least in the short run, would not be to reduce tensions; it might actually increase them.

Why not a referendum?
In view of the self-interest of both Pretoria and Umtata in having Transkei independence widely accepted as an undeniably popular step, and given the peculiar nature of ordinary

Transkei elections, it is indeed surprising that it was not decided to hold a public referendum on the issue. Within white
South Africa there was recent precedent for such a step, for
despite the keen interest of Afrikaner nationalists before
1960 in transforming the Union of South Africa into a republic, it was a point of honor among the ruling National party
after 1948 that this could be done only in consequence of a
public referendum among whites, and not merely by a simple
majority vote in parliament. The referendum was duly held,
of course, in October 1960, with the prorepublican position
carrying by a small margin.

The political value to the Nationalists, at least, of a successful referendum on Transkei independence was suggested
at the time the House of Assembly considered the Status of
the Transkei Bill in May–June of 1976. Although the Progressive Reform party took the unusual step of opposing the bill
at the time of its first reading, during the second-reading
debate Colin Eglin, the PRP leader, stated:

> If a significant majority of the people of the Transkei
> openly express their wish for independence [in a referen-
> dum], we in this party, however much we might differ
> from them in their decision, would not stand in the way of
> their having independence. We will go even further and
> state that under those circumstances we would do every-
> thing in our power to make that independence a success.[20]

The reponse of the minister of Bantu Administration and
Development, M. C. Botha, two days later, was that how the
will of the Transkei people ought to be tested was a matter
solely for Transkei to decide. He continued:

> Did the hon. member want us to intervene there as though
> we were some kind of UN, and hold elections or exercise
> supervision over them? Is the Transkei not to be afforded
> an opportunity of organizing its own affairs itself? May
> they not test the will of their people in their own way?
> This is not our approach to self-determination.[21]

20. *House of Assembly Debates*, June 7, 1976, col. 8369.
21. Ibid., June 9, 1976, col. 8565.

Within Transkei itself, the idea of a public referendum on the independence issue was raised on the floor of the TLA in March 1974 by the leader of the opposition, Knowledge Guzana, at the time the assembly debated a government motion that the cabinet "consider the advisability" of asking Pretoria "to grant full independence to the Transkei within a period of five years."[22] Guzana offered an amendment that would have delayed any such approach until the Transkei government could

> refer the whole subject of independence to the voters of the Transkei, wherever they are, explain the implications of such a constitutional step and seek by way of a referendum the attitude of the people towards independence, and if favourable, obtain a mandate thereto.[23]

Chief Minister Matanzima's reaction to this suggestion was ambiguous, although Guzana's amendment was defeated. He denied the applicability to Transkei of the precedent of the 1960 republican referendum and observed that Swaziland, Lesotho, and Botswana had each become independent from Great Britain without a referendum being held. Moreover, the elections of 1968 and 1973 had already given him a mandate to seek independence, he said. On the other hand, Matanzima gave assurances that his government would "not drag the people of the Transkei into independence if they express the view that they do not want it." "Full consultations" were promised, but he would give no details beyond suggesting that specific bodies—tribal authorities, teachers' associations, the YMCA, and the like—would be sought out, but significantly not the Students' Association. "We cannot consult children on this matter," he said, but his government would approach Transkei citizens in the republic.[24]

Two years later, as the assembly commenced to consider the independence constitution for Transkei, the chief minister reported that the government had in fact consulted with a variety of different tribal and other groups at more than one

22. TLA *Debates, 1974,* p. 69.
23. Ibid., p. 72.
24. Ibid., pp. 91-92.

thousand meetings both inside and outside of Transkei. The result of votes taken at these meetings, according to Matanzima, was 125,424 individuals (or 90 percent) in favor of independence, and 13,945 against.[25] Apart from the fact that this represented a poll of less than 15 percent of the registered Transkei voters in 1973, the details of the vote, in the words of one journalist, stretched "credibility to the limit."[26] For example, 64 percent of the bodies polled failed to produce a single vote against independence. Laurence writes:

> It was not a referendum in the understood sense of the word. General meetings of the different tribes, public bodies and civil service associations were asked to discuss independence and pass resolutions on it. There was no secret vote, only discussion at gatherings of tribesmen organized by pro-Matanzima chiefs equipped with draconian powers or at meetings of civil servants paid by the Transkei government.[27]

It was altogether an unconvincing effort which, far from helping to legitimize the new state, created new suspicions about its popular base. In 1946 no less a figure than General Jan Smuts employed the results of a similar poll among South West African nonwhites as evidence supporting the Union's (ultimately unsuccessful) request to the United Nations for the right to incorporate that territory as a fifth province.[28] Nonetheless, three decades later it is hard to imagine how one could have expected a skeptical and sophisticated world public opinion to have been persuaded by such a plebiscite in Transkei. It was a serious miscalculation, damaging to both the new state and the republic.

Decision-making in Transkei
But if it is arguable that the Transkei electorate did not choose independence, who did? To date, excepting chapter

25. TLA *Debates, 1976,* p. 222.
26. Bill Krige, quoted in Laurence, *The Transkei,* p. 11.
27. Laurence, *The Transkei,* pp. 10–11.
28. Solomon Slonin, *South West Africa and the United Nations: An International Mandate in Dispute* (Baltimore: The Johns Hopkins Press, 1973), p. 78.

10 of D. A. Kotze's book, *African Politics in South Africa,
1964–1974,* there has been no thorough study of the way in
which political decisions have been made in Transkei since
1963. One often encounters, however, the impressionist
conclusion, confirmed by Kotze, that on most issues, and certainly on the issue of Transkei independence, the key personality and perhaps the only personality of note in the territory
has been the chief minister, now the prime minister. Some
observers mention too his younger brother, Chief George
Matanzima, the minister of justice, though merely as an extension of Kaiser. Stories of the Matanzima brothers' dominance of Transkei politics are legion, but one of the clearest
illustrations in public occurred in August 1972 when the
elder Matanzima returned to Transkei after forty-five days in
the United States. Speaking to the waiting press at the East
London airport, obviously before he could report to or consult with his cabinet, let alone the assembly, the chief minister said that based on what he had learned of race relations in
America, the policy of his government would be to grant full
citizenship to whites in an independent Transkei.[29] This
statement represented a reversal of earlier declarations on the
subject. Understandably, the press focused on the substance
of Matanzima's remarks, which was clearly at variance with
the wishes of Pretoria for a racially homogeneous citizenship
in both countries, but it is hard to imagine a more blatant
demonstration of one-man decision-making on an issue of
ideological, if not practical importance.

Regarding the issue of independence, the chief minister
clearly controlled its handling at all stages, although in the
early years of his government this control threatened to lose
him the initiative in the matter. Indeed, when Shadrack
Sinaba, erstwhile chief government whip, moved in the TLA
in April 1966 that the cabinet should ask Pretoria for full
independence for Transkei, George Matanzima entered the
debate to defeat the proposal with an amendment (accepted
49 votes to 1) stating flatly that "the Transkei is not ripe for
independence at this stage."[30] And two years later when the

29. *Daily Dispatch,* August 7, 1972.
30. TLA *Debates, 1966,* pp. 90, 92, 118.

idea of immediate independence was raised again by Cromwell Diko, the chief minister rejected it (supported by all but 2 votes in the assembly) citing cabinet-level negotiations that could not be rushed. However, concurrently he softened this rejection by accepting a motion asking the republican government "to do everything in its power to prepare the Transkei for full independence within the shortest possible time"[31] Later that year TNIP's election manifesto pledged the party generally "to work for complete independence," which was subsequently the basis for Matanzima's claim that the 1968 election results constituted a mandate to seek independence. Yet, at the time, this was not strong enough a commitment for Sinaba and Diko, who ran against TNIP under the banner of the Transkei People's Freedom party but were crushed, their party receiving just 2.4 percent of the total vote.

Four years after this, in May 1972, a motion was again introduced in the TLA that Pretoria be asked to grant independence to Transkei, but this time by the chief minister himself. However, now the independence issue was joined to another request that the republican government cede to Transkei white-owned land in four magisterial districts to its north (Matatiele and Mount Currie) and west (Elliot and Maclear), as well as Port St. Johns, a white enclave on the Indian Ocean.[32] In so many words, Matanzima announced publicly that his government's interest in independence was conditional on Transkei's land claims being satisfied first. Laurence has interpreted the raising of the independence issue by Matanzima at this time and in this way as a last ditch tactical move in his struggle with Pretoria for more land, which had been going on for some years but had reached a moment of crisis only a few days before.[33] The motion carried easily. Thus, over a period of a decade, Matanzima adopted at least three different positions on the sensitive issue of Transkei independence—(1) independence when the territory is "ripe" for it, (2) independence "within the shortest possible time," and (3) independence when, but only when, land claims have

31. TLA *Debates, 1968,* pp. 229, 251, 257.
32. TLA *Debates, 1972,* p. 119.
33. Laurence, *The Transkei,* p. 92

been met—yet maintained his general personal identification with the ideal of independence and his tactical flexibility and increased his electoral support. In terms of political ability, it was a virtuoso performance.

In March 1974 Matanzima finally committed himself on the question. The change from his previous, qualified stance came suddenly in the middle of the month, and this suddenness demonstrated once again Matanzima's proprietary control over political decision-making in Transkei. Until then, the 1972 TLA motion on independence just cited had appeared to stalemate relations between Pretoria and Umtata on this topic. TNIP's 1973 election manifesto declared that a division of the land of South Africa in proportion to population numbers "is basic for the fulfillment of [homeland] independence," and this seemed more significant than the chief minister's passing reference, during the campaign, to the possibility of Transkei independence within five years.[34] At the historic first "summit" meeting in Pretoria on March 6 between Prime Minister Vorster and the leaders of all eight African homelands, Matanzima appears to have joined his counterparts in pressing the point that the existing division of land was unacceptable. Independence for the homelands was also discussed, and Vorster reiterated his view that any of the leaders was free to request independence talks, but in the words of the official communique, "No such request was raised." Of this meeting Laurence has written, "It looked as though he [Matanzima] intended sticking to his stand."[35]

Yet within a week of the ending of the Pretoria summit, the annual conference of TNIP, in closed session and ostensibly responding to resolutions submitted by party members in Cape Town and Johannesburg,[36] reversed the position of the party and endorsed Transkei independence within five years, even without the additional land claimed by Umtata. The single qualification was that taking independence should not "prejudice" Transkei's standing land claims. Laurence

34. *Daily Dispatch,* August 29, 1973; *The Star,* October 24, 1973.
35. *Rand Daily Mail,* March 7, 1974; Laurence, *The Transkei,* p. 95.
36. Kaiser D. Matanzima, *Independence My Way* (Pretoria: Foreign Affairs Association, 1976), p. 65.

quotes Matanzima as saying after this meeting, "This is an historic day. We have decided to go for independence."[37] Then, less than a fortnight later, Matanzima introduced in the TLA the motion on independence referred to earlier, directing the government "to consider the advisability of approaching the Republican Government to grant full independence to the Transkei within a period of five years." Two qualifications were seemingly designed to lessen the appearance that Matanzima had shifted his ground on the relationship between independence and the claim for additional land.

(a) That the land promised to the Transkei in terms of the 1936 legislation of the Union of South Africa be granted to the Territory within a period of five years.

(b) That such a grant [of independence] shall not prejudice the right of the Transkei to the Districts originally claimed.[38]

TNIP as a "consent group"
Matanzima's referral of the independence issue to the 1974 TNIP annual conference before raising the matter in the TLA is interesting and directs our attention to the ruling party's role in the policy-making process. Since it was organized in 1964, TNIP has seemed to aspire to become a nationalist party of the "mass party" type. The "statutes" of the party describe a hierarchical structure of branches, district and regional committees, an annual party conference, and a national executive committee. At levels above the branch, positions are filled by elections from below, presumably to ensure accountability; in order to ensure effectiveness, all members are required to abide by the decisions of the annual conference and the national leadership. Members are also obliged to pay dues of twenty cents per year. Writing of mass parties in French-speaking West Africa nearly two decades ago, Ruth S. Morgenthau observed:

Not all but some of the mass parties had both institutionalized and collective leadership. . . . Elections [of party

37. Laurence, *The Transkei*, p. 95.
38. TLA *Debates, 1974*, p. 69.

leaders] were fairly regular; *elus* and officers gave some account of their stewardship to the members; discipline received serious attention; a predetermined procedure was followed for the making of important decisions.[39]

But this cannot be said of TNIP. In fact, the behavior of the ruling party as well as its "programme of principles" (notably its support for the institution of chieftainship) cause TNIP to resemble not the typical African mass party, but rather, in Morgenthau's terms, a "patron party."[40] In contrast to mass parties, patron parties typically are weakly articulated and have small memberships, limited resources, and functionally a narrow range of activities. They are seldom publicly demonstrative, relying on the local "patrons" for their influence, and are comparatively undisciplined. In TNIP's case, the following points seem relevant:

• Actual party membership has not been large; there were only 3,358 recorded members at the end of 1975, according to the secretary-general's annual report. D. A. Kotze writes that there have been some Transkei constituencies without a single TNIP branch, even a few that are regarded as party strongholds.[41]

• Party finances are meager. In the first quarter of 1975, the central office of TNIP spent just $50.53, exclusive of rent, and the party's bank balance at the end of April was only $444. Moreover, much of the party's income appears to derive from levies on the salaries of party members in the legislature, rather than from membership dues, which it seems are often unpaid. The party has had an unpretentious headquarters in Umtata and at least one paid official, but less than one month before the 1976 elections the party office was closed on each of fifteen visits I paid to it, and the paid official (the secretary-general) was said to be occupied with private business.

39. Ruth Schachter Morgenthau *Political Parties in French-Speaking West Africa* (Oxford: The Clarendon Press, 1964), p. 339.
40. Ibid., pp. 336–41.
41. D. A. Kotze, *African Politics in South Africa, 1964–1974: Parties and Issues* (Pretoria: van Schaik, 1975), p. 110.

• Within Transkei, TNIP has not established links with other voluntary associations, relying instead "on traditional chiefs and headmen for recruitment and support."[42] And, in general, TNIP has made little use of symbols or the paraphernalia of mass activity. Mass meetings have been rare, although not unknown. Even the independence celebrations themselves produced little in the way of special clothing, pictures of leaders, bunting, flags, posters, and the like that have become familiar at independence celebrations elsewhere on the continent.

• Most relevant to this discussion, TNIP has experienced an essentially personal leadership, "unfettered by pre-arranged rules," that Morgenthau states was characteristic of the patron parties she studied.[43] D. A. Kotze writes:

> Ordinary members of the TNIP and members of branch executive committees are under the impression that decisions by the annual congress in respect of policy are binding on the party leadership, and that they can be revoked only by a congress decision. A vague notion exists that the national executive has some sort of final power of review. At higher levels of the party, however, greater weight is attached to the powers of the national executive. . . .

> Within the national executive the cabinet members are the most important, and the cabinet can indeed be regarded as the most important agency for policy formulation, follow-up and execution, and selection of leading persons within the party. Most important within this inner core of the TNIP is the leader, Kaiser Matanzima, who commands the absolute loyalty and trust of the entire leadership. As a result of his strong power basis within the party, his force of personality and intellectual ability, Matanzima is able to obtain his own way without opposition within the congress, the caucus and the cabinet.[44]

David Apter refers to any autonomous body, official or unofficial, whose actual assent to a decision or policy is required

42. Ibid.
43. Morgenthau, *Political Parties*, p. 339.
44. Kotze, *African Politics in South Africa*, pp. 213–14.

before it becomes binding as a "consent group."[45] On paper, TNIP might be thought to be such a body in Transkei, but in fact it is not. Nor are there other entities one can point to that fulfill this role. Decision-making in Transkei is rather characterized by personalized and centralized leadership in the person of the prime minister, Kaiser Matanzima, which has two implications for the future. First, the process of political succession in TNIP and the Transkei government is likely to be unpredictable and confused. And second, the consequences of succession, in policy terms, could be quite sweeping. These points will be taken up in the concluding chapter.

Constitution-making for Transkei
Nothing illustrates so well the Matanzima brothers' dominance of the decision-making process in Transkei as the record of the drafting of the 1976 independence constitution. Formally, three ad hoc bodies were involved. The first to be established was a twenty-seven-member recess committee of the TLA that was created in terms of the motion on independence passed by the assembly on March 27, 1974. The duties of the recess committee were listed in the motion under eight headings, but the first was the most important. The committee was directed to consider "drafting Constitutional proposals to be tabled before the House of Assembly for legislation declaring the Transkei an independent state."[46] (In fact, unlike the 1963 constitution, the 1976 constitution was never reviewed by the House of Assembly in Cape Town. The South African Parliament did enact the Status of Transkei Act, 1976, which declared Transkei independent, but this was not considered by the TLA recess committee.) The motion named the chief minister as chairman of the recess committee. The other members were elected by the TLA on the nomination of the chief minister the next day, one from each of the twenty-six magisterial districts then in Transkei. (Two other districts were joined to the territory in 1975.) They included Chief George Matanzima and all other cabinet

45. David E. Apter, *The Politics of Modernization* (Chicago: University of Chicago Press, 1965), p. 247.
46. TLA *Debates, 1974,* p. 69.

ministers, the leader of the opposition, Knowledge Guzana, and Cromwell Diko.

The second body, whose creation was announced on May 17, 1974, was a "working committee" of experts whose charge it was to examine the constitutional, financial, and administrative aspects of Transkei independence. In fact this committee wrote the new constitution and drafted the many required agreements between the two states. The working committee had six ordinary members, three appointed by each government, and a chairman who was the secretary of the Department of Bantu Administration and Development in Pretoria, I. P. van Onselen, and a deputy chairman. Incongruously, the three representatives of the Transkei government were all white men, but all three were well known to the chief minister. One of them, I. R. Zietsman, was Matanzima's legal adviser.

The third body was a joint cabinet committee of the two governments designed to oversee broad issues of policy at the highest level. Its members were the two Matanzimas, for Transkei; the minister of Bantu Administration and Development, M. C. Botha; Prime Minister John Vorster, acting as chairman; and Daan Potgieter, Pretoria's commissioner-general for Transkei.

The recess committee met twelve times during a period of two years and ultimately issued a three-page report and the draft constitution. Members of the recess committee recall that its early meetings in 1974 were devoted to general discussions of broad constitutional questions: Should Transkei have a bill of rights? Should all members of the legislature be elected? Should the new state follow policies of nonracialism or multiracialism? And who should become Transkei citizens? Subsequently, the recess committee received a full draft constitution, which had been prepared by the committee of experts working from the existing 1963 Transkei Constitution, and considered it in detail. Liaison between the two bodies through this process was effected through Kaiser Matanzima who, though he was not a member of the working committee, is said to have been always fully briefed on its efforts. According to Guzana, however, the draft constitution that was prepared by the working committee did not conform in every respect to the views of the recess committee, and this point was confirmed by Matanzima when the TLA considered section 58, dealing with Transkei citizenship by registration.[47] Indeed, the *Star* reported on June 1, 1976, that the recess committee agreed four times to send back to the working committee the provision in the draft constitution pertaining to citizenship for Xhosa in the cities of South Africa. Still dissatisfied, the recess committee finally decided to amend the draft constitution in this respect at the time it was considered by the TLA. Section 58 was amended on May 18 in a way that suggests the accuracy of this report.

Meanwhile, the joint cabinet committee held three widely spaced meetings. These occurred behind closed doors, and thus little is known of what transpired, apart from the contents of the press release issued at the end of each one. The statements indicated that the meetings were serious negotiating sessions, the first such political bargaining encounters between a South African premier and South African-born black men, save for the March 6, 1974, summit meeting previously cited and a subsequent meeting between Vorster and all the homeland leaders on January 22, 1975. Understandably, the interest of the press in the meetings of the joint cabinet committee was primarily in whether the Matanzima brothers could extract any concessions from Vorster in exchange for their willingness to lead Transkei to independence. Retrospectively, it appears from Laurence's discussion of these meetings that Vorster's willingness to cede Port St. Johns to Transkei and to endorse a racially open citizenship for the territory represented a movement away from his earlier positions, although in the case of Port St. Johns, it is known that the Department of Bantu Administration and Development recommended two years earlier that the white enclave be ceded to Transkei.[48] On the critical issue of the future citizenship of the so-called urban Xhosa, however, Vorster appears to have held fast to his view that these individuals

47. Interview in Umtata, September 13, 1976.
48. Laurence, *The Transkei*, pp. 109–14.

should become Transkeians at independence and, concurrently, cease to be South African citizens. Our interest in these meetings, however, is in the further evidence they give of the tightly controlled process that led to independence and the key role played by Kaiser Matanzima at every step.

Of course, the draft constitution that was finally published on April 23 and tabled in the TLA with the report of the recess committee on May 3, 1976, was considered by the full membership of the TLA between May 4 and May 18, and again briefly on July 26 and 27. At these meetings Matanzima excluded the possibility of discussing the *principle* of independence, arguing that opportunity had existed in March 1974.[49] But the TLA did discuss and pass six amendments to the draft constitution's 76 sections and 11 schedules as it considered them individually, and seven other changes (most of a technical nature) were introduced by the chief minister and accepted without debate on the last day of the TLA's sitting. But only one of the six debated amendments dealt with an issue of great significance (the citizenship of the urban Xhosa), and this amendment was proposed by Matanzima himself, acting on behalf of the recess committee.[50] Altogether, the ratification of the draft constitution by the TLA was a remarkably consentaneous affair, which observers attributed to the unity of the recess committee that Matanzima had skillfully maintained. Even Knowledge Guzana, who had led the fight against independence in 1974 and two years later continued to have reservations, helped shepherd the draft constitution through the assembly, patiently explaining to his colleagues the meaning of various sections and then moving their approval.

In short, while there is indeed a formal correctness to the steps that led to Transkei independence in a legislative sense (apart from the absence of a public referendum), it is hard to demonstrate a deep public longing for it in the territory, although a small minority perhaps could be described as having had such an interest. What seems accurate is that Chief Matan-

49. TLA *Debates, 1976*, p. 224.
50. Ibid., p. 351.

zima himself decided that Transkei independence was desirable in 1976 and then, exploiting his considerable political skills and the powers and prestige of his office, he successfully and adeptly orchestrated a public acceptance of that position, staying uniquely close to the center of decision-making throughout. The title of Matanzima's political auto-biography, published in October 1976, *Independence My Way*, suggests (inadvertently, one may suppose) the chief minister's dominance of the process, the principal conclusion of this chapter. Certainly no national or even urban African leaders were involved at any stage, and very few of the urban African population in any capacity. This may or may not burden the legitimacy of the new state within Transkei itself. Quite clearly it excites suspicions about the process outside Transkei.

One reason for this, it must be said, is Matanzima himself. The nationalist movements of most African countries have in their terminal colonial and early independence periods been dominated by single personalities. Indeed, this may be thought to be the characteristic leadership mode throughout much of contemporary black Africa. What is special about Matanzima is not that he has accumulated a near monopoly of political power in Transkei, but that he has not developed the personal following that has frequently accrued to such leaders. Ali Mazrui writes that almost everywhere in Africa there has been a tendency "to spiritualize the head of state or government in [the] years following independence."[51] Such leadership has been widely described as "charismatic," which in Max Weber's now familiar formulation is itself a basis for system legitimacy. But in these terms, Matanzima is a case apart. He is respected in all quarters for his intelligence, toughness, political adeptness, and singleness of purpose. The facile charge that he is a pliant puppet of Pretoria is rejected by nearly all observers on the scene. Few doubt his sincerity as a Xhosa nationalist. Yet for all of this, he is not personally

51. Ali A. Mazrui, "The Monarchical Tendency in African Political Culture," in Marion E. Doro and Newell M. Stultz, eds., *Governing in Black Africa: Perspectives on New States* (Englewood Cliffs, N.J.: Prentice Hall, 1970), p. 30.

liked or admired outside the territory, and perhaps not even within it, if the writings of journalists and scholars can be taken as a guide. Certainly he is not thought by many to embody in his person the "virtue" or "soul" of his people. In fact, many distrust him, particularly persons outside Transkei.

There are, it seems, several explanations for this estrangement. For example, unlike his counterpart in KwaZulu, Chief Gatsha Buthelezi, Matanzima's personality is cold and aloof. He strikes many observers as arrogant. As a public speaker he is undistinguished. Matanzima has been called politically ruthless, and some have charged that he has at times sanctioned political thuggery on the part of his followers. He has, it appears, been responsible for detention without charge of some of his more extreme critics. (Laurence reports that several attempts have been made on Matanzima's life.)[52] As already seen, some of his policies have varied over time, giving rise to the feeling that his politics have not only been inconsistent but opportunistic. And obviously, Matanzima has lost stature, particularly with international public opinion, by allying himself with the homeland policy of the National party of the republic. The leaders of the seven other homelands have also been stigmatized in the eyes of many by their willingness to take office in structures that would appear to legitimate apartheid in South Africa. But because he was the first to do so and has seemed to embrace Pretoria's homeland policy as a positive good, rather than (as Buthelezi) merely a practical necessity, Matanzima's stigma has been greater than that of the others. The second point in TNIP's "programme of principles" begins as follows:

> 2. It is the purpose of the Party to promote the welfare of the various tribes living in the Transkei through political action, based on the principle of Separate Development.

And upon joining TNIP, a new member is required in terms of the "statutes" of the party to declare:

> I the undersigned, hereby declare that I subscribe to the policy of Separate Development as set out in the Pro-

52. Laurence, *The Transkei*, p. 5.

gramme of Principles of the Transkei National Independence Party, and solemnly undertake to promote its implementation. . . .

There are two additional points. One is Matanzima's support for the institution of chieftainship in Transkei and a continuing and important role for chiefs in the politics of the new state. On September 13, 1975, the *Rand Daily Mail* quoted the chief minister as follows:

> In the Transkei we will forever retain chieftainship. It must be restored in the Transkei if great things are to come. . . . We have observed that the life of any nation centers on the chiefs. . . . It must be the chiefs who are sent to the United Nations and who take part in detente moves. If this is achieved, there will be peace in Southern Africa.

A year later, I. R. Zietsman, who was one of the three Transkei members on the constitutional working committee, reported that although he had advocated that elected members outnumber chiefs in the new Transkei National Assembly, he was overruled by Mantanzima who would agree to nothing more than parity between elected and ex-officio members.[53] Matanzima's view is not surprising from one whose father was a chief, who has himself been a chief since 1940, and who has been one of four paramount chiefs in Transkei since 1966. And of course, one need look no further than Lesotho or Swaziland at the times of their independence to find the institution of chieftainship given place in the "modern" political process. Yet, moving farther afield in contemporary Africa, one finds it generally true that chieftainship, and tribalism with which it is intimately linked, have been regarded as unprogressive, at least among the modern elite. As a practical matter, it is hard to see how, in Transkei, chiefs and their associated tribal structures could be administratively dispensed with for many years. But practical necessity is the least of Matanzima's reasons for supporting chieftainship. In his view the Transkei chiefs are the rightful, God-given leaders of the Xhosa people, not just now but for all time. This causes

53. Interview in Umtata, September 13, 1976.

Matanzima to be seen by nearly all democratic critics of the South African scene as a retrogressive leader who would, to employ Hoernlé's words, push his people "back into an artificial perpetuation of 'primitive' ways."[54]

Finally, there is the imputation of personal gain. Because he was born into the family of a regional chief and became himself a chief at age twenty-five, by the standards of most Transkeians Matanzima has enjoyed a life of privilege, power, and opportunity. An early indication of this was his education at his tribe's expense at Lovedale Institution and the University of Fort Hare. Inevitably, his retention of the post of chief minister, and now prime minister, since 1963 has resulted in additional status, salary ($16,790 per year in 1976–77, making him the best paid of all the homeland leaders), and perquisites. But Matanzima has not hesitated to use his political power to raise himself still further. In 1965 the TNIP-dominated TLA passed a resolution endorsing the elevation of Matanzima from regional chief of Emigrant Tembuland to paramount chief, although this is said to have been of doubtful validity under Tembu tribal law and custom. And on April 13, 1976, the assembly approved the granting of farmland acquired by the Transkei government in terms of the 1936 Land and Trust Act to paramount chiefs and others "who have rendered faithful service in the development of their country."[55] Six days later the East London *Daily Dispatch* reported that

> two farms near Queenstown which were to have formed the basis of a big Transkei Development Corporation cattle ranching project have instead gone to Paramount Chief Kaiser Matanzima and his brother. The farms, which are in the middle of one of South Africa's richest sweet veld farming areas in the Glen Grey district, were bought for more than [$460,000] in January from Mr. A. Wiggill.

As this occurred only a short while before the publication of the draft constitution for Transkei on April 23, it was inevitable that these farms, which were apparently acquired at no

54. Hoernlé, *South African Native Policy*, p. 172.
55. TLA *Debates, 1976*, p. 114.

cost to the Matanzimas, would be seen by many observers as a reward from Pretoria to the chief minister and his brother for their cooperation in the discussion that produced that document. (The minister of Bantu Administration and Development subsequently confirmed in parliament that he had approved that the farms in question go to the Transkei Development Corporation and "that only the dwelling on one of the acquired farms be made available to the Chief Minister.")[56]

Stories in the *Sunday Times* on three successive Sundays in October just before independence charged that the two Matanzima brothers had in fact enjoyed personally profitable and questionable dealings with the South African government for many years. Specifically, the paper alleged that the chief minister had acquired five plots of land from the Bantu Trust for $7,720, for which the Trust had paid a total of about $24,000, and that George and/or Kaiser Matanzima were shareholders in companies that had acquired, since 1968, four Transkei hotels (and their associated liquor trade) from the Bantu Trust for $65,000 less than the Trust had paid for them.[57] Whether or not these transactions were accurately reported, it is clear that in terms of wealth and standard of living the benefits of office have set Matanzima off, and to a lesser extent the members of his cabinet as well, from the great mass of the Transkei population. This difference the prime minister has done little to disguise and certainly nothing to lessen. A contemporary public symbol of this affluence deriving from political power is the row of magnificent mansions constructed just before independence on a hillside on the south side of Umtata for the new Transkei president and senior cabinet members. The presidential mansion, the largest and grandest of all, was reported to have cost $2.3 million when it was handed over as a gift of the South African government on October 19, 1977.

Such social ostentation is, of course, not unusual in the politics of contemporary black Africa and indeed may be expected by the ordinary citizen, in Transkei as elsewhere.

56. *Daily Dispatch,* April 30, 1976.
57. *Sunday Times,* October 3, 10, 17, 1976.

Ali Mazrui sees a partiality on the part of African leaders "for splendid attire, for large expensive cars, for palatial accommodation, and for other forms of conspicuous consumption" as part of the "monarchical tendency in African political culture," which can be supportive of the political system by helping to create "the necessary awe towards authority," required if national integration is to occur.[58] Be that as it may, the fact that Matanzima and his immediate political associates enjoy great material comfort while the mass of Transkeians live perilously close to the "poverty datum line" has created skepticism about his motives and his character on the part of most external observers of Transkei affairs. Accordingly, the legitimacy of Transkei independence, for which he is principally responsible, has suffered, particularly outside Transkei. It is interesting in this connection to speculate as to what difference it might have meant for the acceptability of Transkei independence had Matanzima had the charismatic appeal of a Gatsha Buthelezi, the modern outlook of a Nelson Mandela (who is in fact a distant cousin of the Matanzimas), or the personal humility of an Albert Luthuli. It has been easier to reject Transkei independence because it has been easy to reject Matanzima.

58. Mazrui, "The Monarchical Tendency," p. 32.

4

WHO BENEFITS?

The discussion just concluded of Chief Matanzima's alleged self-interest in Transkei independence directs our attention to a more general question: What are the benefits for Transkeians of being independent, and how are these benefits distributed? The second part of this question rests on the commonplace sociological observation that goods in society are seldom shared equally but are usually distributed in ways that favor certain categories of persons. However, the separatist literature reviewed earlier says little about the distribution of resources within the separated communities after separation has occurred. The concern of these authors is instead with the division of resources between (or among) the separated communities and is obviously based on the danger that separatism could prove to be, in Tiryakian's words, "a European [that is, white] scheme to deprive the blacks of what is [rightfully] theirs." Apart from an equitable division of resources between the races, most of the cited writers appear to see the primary benefit of separatism as the elimination of racial discrimination from the lives of black people (and of the coloureds and the Asians as well) and to conceive of that benefit as being socially indivisible.

The ending of apartheid
The most dramatic accomplishment of Transkei independence is that the territory itself has been purged of apartheid

regulations, although as a matter of practice racial separation in the hotels of Umtata and the post office had quietly disappeared more than a month before. Legally, however, the changeover occurred on October 26. Schedule 11 of the Transkei Constitution, which the National Assembly enacted on that day, lists 122 laws of South Africa that are repealed fully or in part. Among them are such landmark pieces of apartheid legislation as the Reservation of Separate Amenities Act, the Group Areas Act, and the Prohibition of Political Interference Act. Two other well-known apartheid laws that were not listed are the Immorality Act and the Prohibition of Mixed Marriages Act, both antimiscegenation measures, but at independence the minister of justice, George Matanzima, indicated that these would be repealed in time too. Certainly Transkei was not born as a model liberal democracy, as noted above, but with a few trivial exceptions (notably separate schools for whites run, as before, by the Cape Provincial Administration), racial discrimination enshrined in law in Transkei is a thing of the past. Indeed, the independence celebrations themselves were probably the largest mixed-racial gathering ever to have occurred in South Africa up to that time.

The observable effects of this change on the lives of ordinary Transkeians may be hard to see. On economic grounds most Africans in Transkei have had little contact with whites, and in any event race relations in Transkei have always been more open and relaxed than in the urban areas of the republic.[1] Still, in context, it is a change of incalculable importance for African dignity, whose positive consequences for African pride could flow beyond Transkei throughout the region.

The other side of the coin, of course, is that the one million Transkei citizens who are permanently resident in South Africa automatically and involuntarily ceased on October 26 to be South African citizens under the laws of the republic. Since Pretoria will clearly use the Transkei citizenship of these persons as justification for continuing to deny them the full rights of citizenship in the republic, Transkei independence may be assumed to have entrenched racial discrimina-

1. Donald Woods, "Transkei independence: South Africa's calculated risk" *Optima* 25, no. 4 (1975): 215.

tion against them and, by extension, against all Africans in South Africa. Thus, Transkei independence has not produced the general relaxation of race discrimination in the region, even at the level of so-called petty apartheid, that most of the proponents of either partition or federation foresee as the principal benefit and purpose of separatism.

There is one sense in which the effects of racial discrimination continue to be experienced even within the territory, for, as noted earlier, the poverty of Transkei is in part an enduring burden of past racial discrimination. Indeed, many of those who opposed Transkei independence do so precisely because of the belief that it serves to legitimate a division of wealth in southern Africa that is strikingly and unfairly favorable to the interests of the whites. Others have argued that even if this is so, it does not prove that the decision on the part of Transkei to choose independence was wrong, for in the words of Professor Mlahleni Njisane, a one-time naturalized American citizen and the first Transkei ambassador to South Africa, "You cannot give up rights you've never had" (or, by implication, are ever likely to get).[2] There is as yet no indication that Africans in those homelands, such as Kwa-Zulu, that decline independence will be materially better off than Transkeians in the foreseeable future. (Actually, in the short run, the contrary seems the case, for the rate of capital investment in Transkei increased as independence neared. For example, although Transkeians accounted for approximately 77 percent of the combined populations of Transkei and the Ciskei before the transfer of the Herschel and Glen Grey districts in December 1975, as of the end of March 1975, 91 percent of XDC investments in the two areas under the so-called agency agreements program had gone to Transkei.)[3] References to the "birthrights" of Africans in South Africa, which is the vocabulary in which this issue is frequently discussed, assume for the realization of such "rights" a dramatic restructuring of the politics of the republic that cannot yet be foreseen—nor confidently excluded. This is to say that much of the debate concerning the validity of Transkei independence is really an argument about the probable future of

2. Interview in Umtata, September 7, 1976.
3. *Ten Years of Progress*, p. 28.

South Africa, a debate that seems destined to remain inconclusive for some time to come. Be that as it may, it seems necessary to suggest now that the granting of political independence to Transkei ought not to be understood as absolving the whites of the republic from some responsibility for the poverty of the territory, and hence for its material uplift in the future.

Divisible benefits

The sociologist Max Weber posited three dimensions of social inequality: class, status, and power, and it appears to be the case that the divisible benefits of Transkei independence include all three. Specifically, I refer to jobs (and capitalist opportunities for a few) in a locale where most employment is in subsistence farming and unemployment is high, position in an inegalitarian society, and political and bureaucratic authority. Moreover, it is widely agreed that three groups of beneficiaries have derived most of this profit. They are the chiefs, the civil servants, and the new African entrepreneurs.[4] I will now treat each of these groups separately, drawing liberally on the findings of the authors previously cited, though supporting them with new data of my own.

First, however, it seems necessary to qualify an assumption underlying the discussion that follows. The assumption is that the changes in Transkei that I will mention occurred because the Transkei electorate (or at least the Matanzima government) chose political independence for the territory. It is of course very likely that had Matanzima followed instead the path of Chief Gatsha Buthelezi of KwaZulu and refused independence, some of the "benefits" would have been realized anyway. On the other hand, as just indicated in the case of agency agreements, it seems probable that each of the benefits to be discussed has been somewhat greater because Transkei chose independence, although how much greater is clearly impossible to determine. To be precise we can compare independent Transkei only with the territory's previous condition and not with how it might have developed had

4. Charton, "Black Elites"; Kolya Kolbe, "Power and Privilege in a Bantustan—The Transkei," in Glen Moss, ed., *South Africa's Transkei* (Johannesburg, 1976); Southall, "Beneficiaries."

there been different leadership. It would, however, obviously be wrong to attribute all of the changes wholly to the fact of Transkei's becoming independent.

The chiefs. It was indicated earlier that for more than half a century after the annexation of the districts of Transkei, the institution of chieftainship was administratively in eclipse in the territory. In these years, Charton writes,

> the neutralisation of the chiefs was brought about by imposing an administrative grid which did not coincide with the erstwhile chiefdoms, but cut across their boundaries. The essential unit of local government became the "location", in charge of an appointive Black headman, paid by the government.[5]

This removal from substantial administrative responsibility allowed the chiefs in Transkei to retain much of their traditional popularity, but it relegated them to an uncertain role. Altogether, there were just thirty recognized chiefs in Transkei in the middle of the 1950s, according to Hammond-Tooke, each receiving a small stipend from the government.[6]

Had the government of Prime Minister Johannes G. Strijdom in Pretoria (1954–58) behaved as many other central governments in Africa behaved later, the atrophy of the institution of chieftainship in Transkei would simply have been allowed to continue. But this was unacceptable to National party ideology, which held that the chiefs were the "true leaders" of the African people (rather than, for example, the officers of the African National Congress, then still a legal organization). There was also a practical consideration, pointed to by Hammond-Tooke: the council system, which had been introduced in 1895, had not produced effective leadership for the territory. With a few exceptions, the district councillors "seem to have completely failed to present the work of the Bunga [the United Transkeian Territories General Council] in a meaningful way to their constituents."[7]

5. Charton, "Black Elites," p. 62.
6. Hammond-Tooke, *Command or Consensus,* p. 207.
7. Ibid., p. 194.

Thus, in 1956, as noted earlier, the conciliar system was discarded in favor of so-called Bantu Authorities. Administrative boundaries were altered to coincide with tribal boundaries, rather than to cut across them, and at the lowest tier of representation, the tribal authorities, the principle of ascription replaced the principle of election. Recruitment to higher authorities (regional and territorial) was by indirect election. As a result, among the 120 councillors of the Transkei Territorial Authority who accepted "self-government" for the territory in December 1962, 55 were persons who were listed as chiefs and 44 others were individuals listed as headmen. Not surprisingly, the Transkei Constitution of 1963, which they approved, guaranteed that a majority (58 percent) of the membership of the Transkei Legislative Assembly would be chiefs. And thirteen years later the last TLA that accepted the independence constitution had in fact 74 chiefs (60 percent) among a total membership of 123 persons. The new National Assembly has 75 ex-officio chiefs, as noted above. All of which prompts Charton to write:

> Constitutionally speaking the tribal elite, particularly the chiefs, are in a very powerful position. They may dominate the Tribal Authority at the local level, wield considerable influence in the Regional Authorities, and are really in a position to dominate [parliament] if they act in unison with each other.[8]

Obviously the number of recognized chiefs in the territory has increased from the 30 Hammond-Tooke counted in the 1950s. There were at least 64 in 1963, and according to Roger Southall, 96 early in 1974. He has calculated that there were 121 chiefs in Transkei at the time of independence in 1976, although the 1976–77 "Estimate of Expenditure" for the Transkei government includes salaries for only 100. Southall suggests that some of the increase in the number of chiefs after 1974 was the result of TNIP government efforts to purchase support for independence, but he offers no other evidence to support this inference.[9] What is clear is

8. Charton, "Black Elites," p. 63.
9. Southall, "Beneficiaries," p. 13; *T. G. 2-1976*, p. 10.

that a striking growth in the number of chiefs in Transkei has been in progress for two decades. As a result, not all current chiefs can be accommodated as ex-officio members of the National Assembly, and to resolve this problem the 1976 constitution provides (in section 29) for electoral colleges at the district level of all chiefs holding office in order to determine which of their number should sit in Umtata. The constitution specifies that these elections should be held a day earlier than nomination day for candidates for popular election to the National Assembly, presumably so that chiefs who fail to win ex-officio membership can seek to become ordinary members. In fact, 7 chiefs were among the 75 elected members to the first National Assembly in 1976. Two other chiefs failed in the general election.

If the powers of the chiefs have increased, together with their numbers, since the introduction in Transkei of the Bantu Authorities system in the 1950s, so too has their financial stake in existing political arrangements. As late as 1963, some chiefs received as little as $55 annually from the government for the exercise of their official duties. Four years later the minimum pay for a chief had risen to $202, where it appears to have remained until 1974. In that year, however, Matanzima announced that henceforth no chief would earn less than $927 per year, and just a year later this figure was increased to $1,564, or by 68 percent. Note that these are all minimum figures; chiefs with a large number of taxpayers in their areas earned more, up to a maximum of $2,392 more at the time of independence. Moreover, chiefs who sat ex officio in parliament received a further $2,300 in 1976, plus a daily allowance of $9.20. Thus at the time of independence no chief in the National Assembly earned less than $3,360, a figure sixty-one times greater than the minimum stipend for chiefs at the beginning of 1963! Charton's words seem particularly apt here: "The chief then has emerged from the semi-obscurity of the colonial period to inherit the post-colonial kingdom."[10]

10. Charton, "Black Elites," p. 63; TLA *Debates, 1974,* p. 132; TLA *Debates, 1975,* p. 97. In 1976 $1 (U.S.) equaled 0.86956 South African rand.

Civil servants. The first distinctively Transkei bureaucracy came into being as an adjunct of the United Transkeian Territories General Council (known as the Bunga), 1931–56, although estimates of its size during the latter years of this period differ. Charton writes that there were just forty-three African employees of the Bunga in 1953, but R. P. Wronsley suggests a somewhat larger number.

> Legislative powers the "Bunga" had none, but it did have the competence to appoint, promote, discipline and discharge several hundred Bantu clerks, interpreters, agricultural demonstrators, forest guards, roads foremen, lorry-drivers, tractor and grader operators as well as several thousand locally recruited labourers to carry out the work of the District Councils.

Both these authors agree, however, that whatever their number, these Africans were nearly all utilized in subordinate and low-grade positions. Quoting Wronsley, "Most supervisory and all control posts were . . . occupied by Whites—magistrates and other officials of the then Department of Native Affairs." Under the Bantu Authorities system (1956–63), the number of government positions in Transkei filled by blacks increased several fold, but at the beginning of Transkei "self-government" in December 1963, 18.6 percent of the 2,446 positions constituting the "fixed establishment" of the six government departments were still filled by white officers of the Republican Public Service.[11]

If we compare this position with the situation that obtained at the end of 1975, just ten months before independence, three important changes can be seen to have occurred. First, the number of civil service posts in Transkei actually filled by Africans (ignoring temporary vacancies) rose from 1,991 to 11,262 or by 565 percent, not including 16,786 laborers who were also employed at the end of 1975 outside the establishments of the various departments.[12] Indeed, in 1975

11. Charton, "Black Elites," p. 67; R. P. Wronsley, "The Evolution of Public Administration in the Transkei," *Saipa: Journal for Public Administration* 7, no. 1 (March 1972): 5, 9.

12. Republic of Transkei, *Annual Report of the Public Service Commission, 1976,* p. 3.

alone, the number of African civil servants in Transkei nearly doubled, increasing by 94 percent. Not all of this growth, of course, represented new posts; some of it is accounted for by the transfer to the jurisdiction of the Transkei government of activities previously controlled by South Africa (for example, police and prisons), or in the case of nine mission hospitals taken over in 1975, by private entities. But there were many new posts, reflecting toward the end of this period the impending growth at independence in the number of government ministries from eight to eighteen. A few of these new ministries, for example, the Public Service Commission, were in fact former subdepartments which had merely been upgraded; but others, notably the Departments of Defence, Information, Foreign Affairs, and Posts and Telegraphs, had no counterparts in the government of a dependent Bantustan. Independence thus increased the number of government jobs in Transkei dramatically.

The second change was in salaries. During the thirteen years of Transkei "self-government," salary scales for the Transkei Public Service were upgraded nine times—1964, 1967, 1968, 1969, 1970, 1971, 1972, 1973, and 1974, so that counting normal incremental increases, the ordinarily competent civil servant would have enjoyed no fewer than twenty-two pay raises during this period.[13] As a result, in 1976-77 it was projected that salaries, wages, and allowances to civil servants and teachers would consume 30.3 percent of the Transkei budget. These officials continue to earn less than whites filling equivalent positions in the republic (Transkei's few diplomats appear to be an exception to this pattern), and an awareness of this differential has resulted in repeated bitter complaints in the TLA.[14] Nonetheless, in 1976-77 the salary range for a grade II clerk was $1,346 to $2,415, while an artisan working for the Department of Roads and Works earned between $1,863 and $3,105 annually. Remembering that in 1973 the per capita income in Transkei was just $201, if the earnings of the migrant workers are included, we see

13. Wronsley, "The Evolution of Public Administration," p. 14; Charton, "Black Elites," p. 68.
14. See, for example, TLA *Debates, 1976*, p. 56 ff.

that even these incomes for posts in the lower reaches of the Transkei bureaucracy must have been attractive. Furthermore Charton notes that one consequence of the manpower bottleneck resulting from the enlargment of the civil service and the scarcity of qualified personnel outside the bureaucracy has been a system of rapid internal promotions based on in-service training. Promotion rates, she writes, rose steadily, from 2.2 percent in 1964 to 13 percent in 1975.[15] Clearly, in a region that has traditionally experienced low incomes and widespread unemployment, a finite population of some 11,000 African civil servants has obtained, concurrent with the territory's move to independence, an appreciable improvement in its economic position.

The third change, which has been referred to in chapter 2, is that the number of republican officials seconded to the Transkei government decreased absolutely by 34.8 percent, from 455 in 1963 to 292 in 1975, and of course more dramatically as a percentage of the total "fixed establishment" of Transkei—18.6 percent to just 2.5 percent. In 1976 the absolute number of seconded white officials rose again, to 358 at the end of the year, but this was a lower percentage still of the whole Transkei civil service, 2.1 percent. The significance of these developments is that an increasing number of high-level positions were opened up for African incumbency. This and the concurrent increase in the absolute number of high-level positions resulting from the aforementioned growth in the number of ministries have permitted—indeed required—the emergence of a group of comparatively well-paid, high-status African bureaucrats in Transkei, numbering perhaps several hundred persons altogether. These officials, too, continue to earn less than their white counterparts elsewhere. Nonetheless, in 1976–77 the black secretary of education in Transkei earned $12,420. The secretary of the Public Service Commission and eleven departmental assistant secretaries each earned not less than $8,073. And I have counted 162 other positions in the 1976–77 "Estimates" that were occupied by Africans, not including the cabinet ministers themselves, in which the minimum annual salary was $5,451

15. Charton, "Black Elites," p. 68.

or more, in context a princely income. Certainly this group's
stake in independence cannot be doubted.

Two other groups also receive salaries from the Transkei
government, although these individuals are not usually
thought of as civil servants. One group consists of members
of parliament. Already treated have been the chiefs, who are
ex-officio members of the new National Assembly, but there
are seventy-five others who owe their seats to popular election. At the beginning of the TLA in 1964, elected members
received $920 per annum exclusive of sessional allowances.[16]
By 1974–75 the figure had risen to $2,180, and in the penul-
timate year of "self-government" it was raised again to
$3,450, or on that occasion by 58 percent, while the sessional
allowance was concurrently increased from $5.75 to $9.20
per day.[17] Within the full membership of the National Assembly, of course, those who are the most favored financially
are the ministers. I have previously noted that in 1976–77 the
chief minister received a salary of $16,790, not including an
expense allowance of $1,380. Ordinary ministers received
$13,915 per annum, plus an allowance of $1,035. Various
other officials of the TLA (chairman, whips, and so forth)
received nominal increments above their salaries as members.
It seems evident, therefore, that as time has gone on, the
financial rewards of parliamentary office have increased for
all MPs relative to economic opportunities for the population generally, particularly for elected members, and most
especially for the cabinet ministers.

The second group consists of teachers, all but less than 1
percent of whom are now employed in government schools.
Charton has described the teaching profession for Africans in
Transkei much earlier in the colonial period in strikingly
negative terms.

> They [the African teachers] were poorly educated, and
> poorly paid too. Thus when compared with the Whites
> they stood low in the hierarchy of educational and eco-
> nomic status. The dominant colonial society did not
> accept them as equals for these, as well as racist reasons. In

16. TLA *Debates, 1974,* p. 130.
17. TLA *Debates, 1975,* p. 97.

a very real sense they . . . were 'men in the middle', with aspirations which bent them towards their colonial masters and with qualifications which alienated them from their fellows without commending them to the dominant society.

But, she writes, after 1963 teachers in Transkei "gained tremendously from the policies pursued by the Matanzima Government."[18] The increased importance attributed by the government to their role is suggested by the steadily increasing proportion of Transkei budgets devoted to education. In 1964-65 the Department of Education absorbed 11.3 percent of total expenditures of the Transkei government.[19] By 1971-72 the equivalent figure was 20.4 percent, and in 1975-76 it was 21.8 percent. Concurrently, as one would expect, the number of African teachers in Transkei grew. Wronsley states that there were about 4,000 African teachers in Transkei at the end of 1964.[20] By 1973 the number had grown to more than 8,000, and in 1976-77 the budget called for salaries for 9,459 African teachers, not including 2,806 principals and vice-principals. Salary levels also improved. In 1976-77 the average salary of the 9,459 teachers was $1,554, although in an era in which there is increasing concern with sex discrimination, it is interesting to note that the average salary for women teachers in Transkei at this time was $988 less than the average salary of men teachers, of which there were 1,969. At independence, teachers thus ranked economically well above the peasant farmers, who are the largest occupational group in the population, and were on a par with the lower echelons of the civil service. Charton reports that the public image of teachers in Transkei is a poor one because of the alleged drunkenness and professional incompetence of many, and the government has actively worked to keep teachers politically submissive, doubtless because it recognizes that a "fairly strong anti-TNIP attitude" exists among them.[21] In material terms, however, they too are clearly favored in the new state.

18. Charton, "Black Elites," p. 65.
19. *Transkei: Economic Revue, 1975,* p. 68.
20. Wronsley, "The Evolution of Public Administration," p. 9n.
21. Charton, "Black Elites," p. 67; Kotze, *African Politics in South Africa,* p. 207.

African entrepreneurs. Although the bartering of economic goods did occur on an irregular basis among the Cape Nguni prior to their contact with white men, the specialized role of trader was not found among these traditional societies.[22] Leo Kuper writes, "The concept of the independent businessman, as of the wage earner, was a product of culture contact."[23] But this contact, in the case of Transkei, also brought white traders, who soon established among themselves a near monopoly over the buying of produce and the selling of manufactured goods.[24] In 1922 Proclamation No. 11 reinforced this monopoly by stipulating that a minimum distance of five miles should separate trading stores. This ruling had the effect of thwarting the development of African competitors of the white traders, ostensibly in the interests of preventing "overtrading." In 1934 Proclamation No. 244 relaxed the five-mile radius rule to two miles. Gillian Hart reports that even this restriction was resented by Africans in Transkei. Still, between 1936 and 1952 the number of African general dealers in Transkei and the Ciskei combined increased from just 19 to 206. However, African general dealers were only 17.2 percent of the total in the two areas as late as 1952.[25]

Hart dates the first official efforts to assist African businessmen as 1959, although half a decade earlier the Department of Native Affairs had made it policy to freeze the rights of white traders in all the African areas.[26] In 1959 Pretoria established the Bantu Investment Corporation and charged it with responsibility for helping to promote, through provision of capital, technical advice, and other means, African entrepreneurship in the reserves. Six years later these activities concerning the Ciskei and Transkei were taken over by a new

22. Isaac Schapera, ed., *The Bantu-Speaking Tribes of South Africa* (London: Routledge and Kegan Paul, 1937), pp. 153–54.
23. Leo Kuper, *An African Bourgeoisie: Race, Class, and Politics in South Africa* (New Haven: Yale University Press, 1965), p. 262.
24. Charton, "Black Elites," p. 69.
25. Gillian P. Hart, *Some Socio-Economic Aspects of African Entrepreneurship, With Particular Reference to the Transkei and Ciskei* (Grahamstown, South Africa: Institute of Social and Economic Research, Rhodes University, 1972), pp. 95, 109.
26. Ibid., p. 96.

entity, the Xhosa Development Corporation, set up in accordance with the republic's Bantu Homelands Development Corporation Act, No. 86, of 1965. By 1975 the BIC and XDC together had made 949 loans in Transkei totaling $8,586,597 in value. The following specific accomplishments of these loans were noted in the XDC's tenth annual report, entitled *Ten Years of Progress.*

1. A total of 474 trading stations in Transkei that had previously been owned by whites had passed to African owners, while 88 other trading stations had been acquired by the XDC in anticipation of future transfer to African owners.

2. African managers had been established in 29 of Transkei's 50 hotels, and in six of the territory's 8 independent bottle stores.

3. Loans had been made to 57 African bus operators.

4. Africans already owned 18 of the 32 garages taken over from white owners. Another 5 garages still owned by the XDC had African managers.

5. Undergirding all of these ventures, the XDC had organized training programs and other special services to maximize the chance of success on the part of these new African entrepreneurs.

In short, during a period of sixteen years (1959-75), about 532 black Transkeians had been assisted in securing ownership of, or management responsibilities in, a variety of small-scale enterprises. This level of achievement, which for such a period can only be described as modest, is partially explained by the lack of entrepreneurial training among Transkei Africans and the extraordinarily limited amount of private capital available in the territory.[27] Since both of these constraints are intractable, the XDC has followed two additional courses of action in order to promote the economic development of the territory. The primary justification for these, at least in the short run, is not that they result in increased African

27. J. Venter, "Financial and Capital Aid to the Private Sector with Special Reference to the Xhosa Development Corporation, Ltd.," in W. Backer, ed., *The Economic Development of the Transkei* (Alice: Lovedale Press, 1970), p. 87.

entrepreneurship (although in the longer run this is hoped for), but that they increase the number of jobs available in the territory.

The first of these strategies (from the standpoint of the time of its inauguration) has been for the XDC (and since April 1, 1976, the Transkei Development Corporation as its successor in Transkei) to purchase from white owners, or indeed to establish itself, undertakings deemed important for the economic development of Transkei. Because of their cost or complexity, these undertakings cannot be turned over to African owners or managers for the time being, and thus are operated by the TDC itself. In fact, it seems unlikely that some of these enterprises can ever be sold to private African owners because of the amount of capital that would be required. Thus, what is probably emerging in Transkei is a form of permanent state capitalism under the control of the TDC. It is therefore interesting that until recently all of the members of the board of Directors of the XDC/TDC were white men appointed by the minister of Bantu Administration and Development in Pretoria. Currently, the board consists of five whites and five black Transkeians, three of whom are TNIP MPs.[28] Examples of the kinds of ventures that are now owned by the TDC are Transkei Hilmond Weavers and the Vulindlela Furniture Factory in Umtata; the Transkei Hotel, also in the capital; two decorticating plants; two quarries, at Butterworth and Umtata; a dairy; and an irrigation project at Qamata. The annual turnover of all these undertakings combined in 1974–75 was $49,309,530, representing an increase of 371 percent over the equivalent figure for 1969–70, just five years before. In early 1975 these XDC-owned firms in Transkei employed 4,730 Africans, one-third of them in the construction field.

The second strategy of the XDC/TDC was and is the encouragement of so-called "white agency" investment. In 1955 the Commission on the Socio-Economic Development of the Bantu Areas (the Tomlinson Commission) recommended that, in order to expedite the creation of employment opportunities in these areas, white capitalists should be

28. *Daily Dispatch*, June 14, 1976.

permitted to invest inside the African homelands. But the government of the day feared that such investment would thwart its policy of separate development and therefore disapproved the suggestion, a prohibition that remained in force until the death of Prime Minister H. F. Verwoerd in September 1966. Shortly thereafter, however, responding to the manifest inadequacy of the existing policy to foster the desired economic growth in the homelands, the government in 1968 lowered the barriers to white capital entering the reserves under controlled conditions. Two of these conditions were the most important: Whites could not own land in the homelands, they could only lease it. And white industrialists would have to agree to sell their interests back to local black businessmen (or, in the case of Transkei, to the TDC) after a stipulated period. To advance this program, Pretoria announced in 1970, as related earlier, a number of artificial economic incentives ("concessions") to white investment in the homelands designed to outweigh the obvious economic disincentives. These concessions included, and still include, low-interest loans, factories built by the corporation to specification and made available at reasonable rentals, and rebates on the cost of transporting goods out of Transkei by railroad. Compared with the other ventures of the XDC/TDC, the white agency program has been highly successful. Even Southall, who is no apologist for separate development, allows that "claims made by the Development Corporation that it has received a flood of inquiries about industrial opportunities [in Transkei] are not just propaganda." Charton provides figures which show that in just two years ending in 1976 the number of white agency firms in Transkei increased from seventeen to twenty-nine, representing an increase in total "white agency" investment (including XDC/TDC loans) from $13.5 million to $51.6 million.[29]

There is, however, one additional incentive to external investment in Transkei that does not appear on official listings: the low wages paid to African workers. In 1976 an African seamstress working among hundreds of others in a modern clothing factory in Butterworth told me that she earned just

29. Southall, "Beneficiaries," p. 20; Charton, "Black Elites," p. 70.

$1.15 for an eight-hour workday, and such a wage-rate
appears to be representative. It is far lower than what she
would earn in Johannesburg. The Matanzima government
appears to accept the need for low wages at this stage in
Transkei's development. Southall notes that it has refused to
enact minimum-wage legislation and opposes the emergence
of trade union activity in the territory.[30] I estimate that up
to 1976 the white agency program alone had resulted in the
creation of about 9,000 new industrial jobs in Transkei,
which in a region of chronic high unemployment may be
grounds for satisfaction on the part of the individuals who
have found work. Yet clearly, most of these positions are
very low paying, so that the material benefit to these persons
is circumscribed. Indeed, an appreciation of this could produce feelings of resentment among these workers based on
the sense of being exploited for the benefit of others. I note
Charton's reference to the emergence of a new "have not"
class of African workers in Transkei, who in time could make
common cause with the African peasantry. "When," she
writes, "Black industrialists take over from White agency industries, or from the corporation, they will inherit an alienated labour force."[31]

Abhorrence of race discrimination is not the only conceivable
reason for advocating race separatism in southern Africa. One
can imagine an individual who is insensitive to the moral evil
of race discrimination, but who nonetheless embraces separatism as a means of avoiding the possible consequences of discrimination in southern Africa—political instability, violence,
and the end of what some refer to as the "European way of
life" there. Yet, from hints in their writings that I have reviewed, it seems clear that all, or certainly most, of the
authors cited previously have come to their consideration of
separatism (not all, of course, have accepted separatism) from
a personal commitment to the cause of racial justice and to
liberal democracy generally. This is obviously the case with
R. A. Hoernlé, Denis Cowen, Gwendolen Carter, and the sig-

30. Southall, "Beneficiaries," p. 19.
31. Charton, "Black Elites," p. 71.

natories of the SPRO-CAS report, to mention only a few.
Thus, while none of the fourteen statements I have dealt with
treats at length the possible benefits of separatism (partition
or federation) other than (1) the transfer of control of appreciable material resources from whites to Africans and (2) the
ending of racial discrimination, it may not be unfair to these
authors to infer that they also have other benefits of separatism in mind, which loosely correspond to elements of what
Lucian Pye has called the "development syndrome."[32] These
benefits are political and social equality, recruitment to political office on the basis of achievement norms rather than
ascription, pluralistic democracy, and African economic independence. The benefits of Transkei independence will now be
considered under these headings.

Equality. The first point obviously is that independence
has rid Transkei of the scourge of blatant, official race discrimination. Considering how much international criticism of
South Africa in recent decades has focused on offensive signs
of racial exclusion that have traditionally been attached to
amenities in that country, I find it odd that the elimination
of these in Transkei has gone seemingly unappreciated. In
principle this step toward legal universalism should benefit
every African in the territory, but clearly its effect on the
African elite of Transkei, whose contact with whites is
greater, will be more substantial.

Materially speaking, however, there can be no question but
that the recent changes associated with independence have
inordinately benefited a tiny percentage of the population.
When all the groups and individuals I have previously mentioned as having profited in jobs and/or income are added together, their number is still only 35,172, just 1.5 percent of
the de facto population of the country. And within this
group there is a much smaller number of chiefs, high-level
civil servants, elected MPs, managers, and entrepreneurs, totaling perhaps 1,000 persons altogether, whose material benefit
has been far greater than the rest. These are the most obvious

32. Lucian Pye, *Aspects of Political Development* (Boston: Little,
Brown, 1966), p. 45.

beneficiaries of Transkei independence, again materially speaking. Indeed, from an economic point of view it perhaps could be argued that Transkei independence has increased inequalities in Transkei rather than the reverse, at least among Africans, raising the few rather than the many. Still, the greater economic equality of the past among Africans was the equality of near universal poverty. In short, Transkei independence has fostered individual equality in a legal and symbolic sense, the importance of which should not be downgraded from the standpoint of human dignity. Materially, however, the lives of most Transkeians have so far remained unchanged.

Recruitment norms. Concern with the norms governing recruitment for political office is obviously but another manifestation of the issue of equality. Here, from the standpoint of the vast literature on modernization and political development, the entrenchment of the institution of chieftainship in Transkei is a profoundly retrogressive step. There are, of course, fewer chiefs proportionately in the new National Assembly than there were in the TLA after 1963, but this difference is trivial compared with the substantial role provided for chiefs under the new constitution. It is not unknown, of course, for chiefs to have risen to high office in many of the new states of tropical Africa, but in nearly all of these cases the individuals in question sought popular support through direct elections. Chief Matanzima has never stood in such an election. And while it is hard to imagine dispensing altogether with the services of the chiefs in the administration of Transkei, at least in the short run, it does not seem necessary to have granted them as powerful a role in the central government as they now have. Clearly, the continuing importance of ascriptive norms in Transkei politics depreciates the value of Transkei independence in the eyes of much of the world.

Pluralism. Although many of the benefits arising from recent developments in Transkei reflect in some measure the structural differentiation of Transkei society, many authors have noted the political dependence of nearly all members of the new Transkei elite on the government and more particularly on the ruling party. Structural differentiation has not, save perhaps within the bureaucracy, produced a number of centers of political power that, through competition among them, might be said to be moving Transkei toward a form of pluralistic democracy. Instead, Transkei politics would seem to resemble a political oligarchy focused on Chief Matanzima and his close advisers. The chiefs are dependent on the goodwill of the government for their political positions, especially now that not all of them can be accommodated in the National Assembly. All but a small number of the elected members of the assembly are TNIP supporters. Teachers and civil servants, paid by the government, have had impressed upon them the importance of their political subordination to the cabinet.[33] And African businessmen, who might be thought to represent a potential countervailing pressure to the political elite, are typically dependent on an official corporation for funding and training. Indeed, the weakest link in the Transkei oligarchy would seem destined to be relations between the government and the executive of the TDC, which will bear watching. Charton notes that the only group of elite members from whom some independence of thought might be expected are the lawyers in private practice, ministers of religion, and other professionals who are self-supporting. Yet the number of these individuals is small, minuscule if the clergymen are excluded, and their past record of political activity is unimpressive.[34]

Economic independence. Finally, despite the initial efforts of the Bantu Investment Corporation and later the XDC/TDC to foster the emergence of a class of African businessmen in Transkei, the magnitude of that effort has not been great, and almost none of the individuals directly affected thereby gained control over the utilization of productive resources. Most have become petty traders with the opportunity to sell only merchandise produced elsewhere, usually by whites. In

33. Charton, "Black Elites," pp. 66, 69.
34. Ibid., pp. 71–72.

terms of the development of industry within Transkei, it seems clear that the prime impetus has become, and will continue to be, the white agency agreements negotiated with the Development Corporation. And while these agreements are nominally intended to result in eventual black ownership of industry in Transkei, there can be little doubt that short of expropriation by the Transkei government (against which risk the white agents are in fact protected by guarantees of compensation by Pretoria), most of these factories will continue to be owned by white capitalists in the republic and elsewhere, a permanence of white interests in Transkei that was in fact anticipated by Pretoria in 1974.[35] In short, the economic development of the territory, which relatively although not absolutely has made impressive strides in the current decade, particularly in the two growth points of Butterworth and Umtata, is linking the Transkei economy ever more closely with the capitalist economy of the republic. It is a linkage that rests squarely on the availability of cheap African labor, over which Transkeians have heretofore exercised virtually no control because of the accountability of the XDC/TDC solely to Pretoria. Meanwhile, the imperative of labor migrancy continues, substantially unaffected by any of the foregoing. It cannot be said, therefore, that the economic changes that have been associated with Transkei independence have enhanced the economic freedom of the territory; they have made it only a little less of an economic backwater. Indeed, given the far greater economic strength of the republic, it is difficult to see how any of the peripheral territories, the so-called BLS countries no less than Transkei, could escape a substantial economic dependency on the industrial heartland, no matter who is in power in Pretoria and what their economic policies are. Excluding the possibility of substantial investments in Transkei from outside the region, it seems evident that the Transkei economy will be a subordinate part of the capitalist economy of the subcontinent, as long as that economy survives.

But if the quality of the benefits of Transkei independence and their distribution among the citizens of the new state fail

35. *Survey of Race Relations, 1974*, p. 215.

in a number of important respects to produce that African "liberation," even within the territory, that would seem to be the goal of much separatist writing, these benefits have nonetheless given a small class of Africans a definite stake in the Transkei status quo and indirectly in nonrevolutionary change (as against revolutionary change) in the republic. Southall has referred to this as a "class alliance between privileged social groups in the Transkei and white South Africans" and has speculated that such a development, reproduced in the other homelands as well, could in time result in the white industrial heartland of South Africa being surrounded by a ring of politically conservative, economically satellite black states. He suggests that such a development could "extend the future of white supremacy in the subcontinent," although he is surprisingly vague regarding the process.[36]

This reference to a biracial class alliance is reminiscent of Heribert Adam's earlier (1971) suggestion that, contrary to the expectations of many observers, South African society as a whole could move by evolutionary means and mutual accommodation (although not without great pressures and some violence) to a new and stable class basis of social stratification, instead of a blatantly racist one.[37] But Adam's idea of a biracial alliance within a property-owning class is not limited spatially to the country's rural areas; indeed, it would have a major expression in the cities. In contrast, Southall's African bourgeoisie is found only in the homelands. This seems a critical difference. White South Africa has an obvious interest in secure borders; but the essence of its security problem, as the urban riots of 1976 and 1977 have again shown, lies in the urban townships, apparently beyond any immediate effect or benefit from Transkei independence. Transkei independence has fostered political stability where it was not really lacking; conversely, independence has failed to promote such stability where its absence seems truly to threaten the survival of the existing political and social system.

36. Southall, "Beneficiaries," pp. 22–23.
37. Heribert Adam, *Modernizing Racial Domination: The Dynamics of South African Politics* (Berkeley: University of California Press, 1971), chap. 6.

5

THE FIRST YEAR

Although intense preparations for Transkei independence
began many months before the event and were carried forward with a dogged thoroughness characteristic of the South
African bureaucracy, anomalies inevitably existed after October 26. For example, for some weeks the city council of the
capital city consisted only of white men, none of whom appear to have been Transkei citizens. (Interestingly, Transkei
citizenship is not a criterion for voting in elections to public
bodies at the local level, or for being a candidate in such elections. But conversely, in terms of the Immovable Property
Control Act of 1977, persons who are not citizens may not
acquire immovable property unless they first receive the approval of the minister of Land Tenure [5/31].)[1] Predictably,
therefore, a continuing theme of official decisions during the
first year of independence concerned the elimination of these
anomalies, such as the dropping in November of inappropri-
ate South African holidays, for example, Settlers' Day and
the Day of the Covenant (11/10). Regarding the Umtata City
Council, the *Daily Dispatch* reported on December 3 that the
central government had appointed four black councillors to

1. Dates in parentheses or brackets (month/day) in the text refer to
issues of the *Daily Dispatch* for the period October 26, 1976, to October 25, 1977, unless indicated otherwise.

98

this body, but blacks still remained a minority of the total membership until the first municipal elections nine months later. Then a racially balanced slate—five Africans and five whites—calling itself "the trusted ten" was swept into office. (Despite reported apathy on the part of white voters, a white candidate actually topped the poll.) And a few days later, but nearly eleven months after independence, Umtata had its first African mayor, Zacharia Mbuque, who had previously been one of the four appointed black councillors (9/9).

Naturally, public attention on changes in Transkei focused on the sensitive field of race relations. Thus the formation in early January of a seemingly innocuous body, the Transkei Life Saving Association, justified a small news story, presumably because it was connected with the nonracial use of public swimming baths (1/7). At the end of the first regular session of the National Assembly in June, Peter Kenny, the resident reporter in Umtata for the *Daily Dispatch,* summarized the work of the session under the headline, "Barriers gone, bans remain" (6/15). But a few color barriers were not eliminated. In terms of an agreement between the Transkei and South African governments, hospitals in Umtata and Butterworth maintained their whites-only sections for the use of seconded officials and their families (1/8), and similarly, in Umtata two white schools continued to exist under the control of the Cape Provincial Administration. (An exception was made in one of these schools when the three children of the Transkei finance minister, T. T. Letlaka, were enrolled. The three youngsters had received their previous education in Britain, where their father had been a political exile, and they could not speak Xhosa.) These vestiges of the former apartheid order do not appear to have sparked political controversy, but another that did during the first year of independence was the retention of the Immorality Act, which proscribes sexual intercourse between whites and blacks. Although the justice minister, George Matanzima, promised at independence to repeal this statute (10/30) and the related Prohibition of Mixed Marriages Act, this was not done by May when, notwithstanding the acknowledged nonenforcement of these laws, the National Assembly on its own resolved unanimously that the Immorality Act should be scrapped.[2]

In the field of education the 1977–78 budget estimate for the Department of Education provided another indication of change. The figure, $47.9 million, was 67.5 percent larger than for the preceding year, although as a percentage of the total budget (now covering eighteen departments rather than just seven) it was essentially unchanged. Some of this increase was doubtless linked to the government's plans for compulsory education for all children to Standard II (grade 4), which were announced by the minister of education, W. S. Mbanga, in April. Minister Mbanga also said the way school subjects had been taught in Transkei would have to be changed to account for the achievements of national heroes and martyrs (4/13).

In May the one-time Umtata branch of the University of Fort Hare (the main campus of which is located near Alice in the Cape Province) was formally opened as the new University of Transkei, and Prime Minister Matanzima was installed as its first chancellor. Concurrently, construction began on the first phase of the university's new campus, which alone was expected to cost $15.1 million. Since in the middle of 1977 the university had just 6 full-time students (in addition to 288 part-time students, 7 of whom were white), the motive behind these decisions was clearly one more of national prestige than of educational necessity (4/6).

Six months earlier, in a matter related to the University of Transkei, an event occurred that simultaneously revealed the sorry state of "women's liberation" in the territory and the legislative power of the prime minister. On November 9, 1976, with the elder Matanzima absent, the National Assembly successfully demanded that the government remove a provision from its University of Transkei Bill that allowed women staff members of the university to be dismissed if they married. But six days later the prime minister returned to parliament to compel a reversal of this decision, which had been virtually unanimous. The *Daily Dispatch* quoted the prime minister's statement of his social philosophy on this

2. *Debates of the National Assembly, 1977*, p. 394.

point as follows, which seems sufficiently divergent from
contemporary Western trends to bear repeating (11/16).

> When a woman married, she took up a new profession,
> he said. But people wanted the Government to go on em-
> ploying her. This would result in the university being
> flooded by professors' wives.
> "Our children who leave university fully qualified will
> find their way blocked by these old hags.
> "And when this lady gets pregnant, she has to apply for
> leave. Is the State going to pay for a person who gets sick
> on her own volition?"

Political freedom
Although narrowly the term *apartheid* merely refers to statu-
tory racial discrimination in South Africa, increasingly the
word conjures up images not only of racial discrimination but
also of the political repression of persons and organizations
who would protest and oppose that discrimination. Certainly
South Africa is today nearly as well known in the world for
its panoply of security laws as it is for its race legislation.
And while many of the governments that berate South Africa
at the United Nations are even less tolerant of dissent at
home than is the republican government, the Western critique
typically rests on the hope, if not the expectation, that once
apartheid has been eliminated from South Africa, liberal
democratic forms should be possible there too. In this view,
African emancipation should mean not only freedom from
racial discrimination, but political freedom generally. Accordingly, there has been much interest in whether or not political freedom would flourish in an independent Transkei.

First indications were not promising. Earlier I mentioned
the detentions under Proclamation R400 of many of the
leaders of the opposition Democratic party at the end of July
1976. The detainees included the party leader, Hector
Ncokazi, together with the party treasurer, S. A. Xobololo
(a member of the TLA who was reportedly scheduled to
introduce shortly thereafter an amendment to the citizenship
clauses of the Transkei Constitution), and its national chairman, Jackson B. Nkosiyane. In August the deputy leader,

O. O. Mpondo, and the general secretary, W. D. Pupuma, were similarly arrested. At independence all of these individuals and perhaps a dozen others (not all members of the Democratic party) were still in jail. Some journalists in Umtata at the time of independence speculated that Matanzima might mark the occasion by declaring a general amnesty, for in August he had denied personal responsibility for the arrest of the DP leaders (8/10/76). But no such announcement was made. Two detainees who were released just before independence (and deported) after spending fourteen days in jail were John Kani and Winston Ntshona, the internationally known actors. Both were alleged to have made vulgar and inflammatory statements on stage during a Butterworth performance of the Athol Fugard play, *Sizwe Banzi is Dead,* in which they starred. Predictably these arrests immediately resulted in worldwide protests and demonstrations involving many celebrated names of the international theatrical community. From the standpoint of Transkei public relations, no more damning and inept use of police power can be imagined than the detentions of Kani and Ntshona when they occurred.

On November 10 the *Daily Dispatch* reported that nine more persons had been detained under Proclamation R400, including Peter Nkosiyane, a member of the new National Assembly and a leading figure in the newly formed Transkei People's Freedom party. The next day the paper said that, altogether, twenty-four individuals were being detained. Thereafter, every month or so brief newspaper reports appeared recording the release of detainees ("Transkei Frees Four") and the arrest—and in one case the rearrest— of others ("Maluti Leader Held in Transkei"), all under Proclamation R400 until June 1977, when it was repealed and superseded by the Transkei Public Security Act.

Not only did the Transkei government thus initially continue to apply against some of its own citizens the extraordinary and arbitrary police powers it inherited from its predecessor regime, but in at least two cases it appeared willing after independence to enforce preindependence security judgments of the South African authorities. On February 22, Phumzile Majeke, a one-time member of the executive of the "black consciousness" South African Students Organization

(SASO), was arrested in Umtata on grounds that he had contravened a 1975 banning order that confined him to the
Qumbu magisterial district (in Transkei) until October 31,
1978. According to the *Daily Dispatch,* a friend "said he
[Majeke] was asked why he had contravened the restriction
orders placed on him and he said he thought the orders had
become invalid when Transkei attained independence."
Majeke was directed by the Transkeian authorities to return
to Qumbu and not leave again without first getting permission of the local magistrate.

The second instance involved five Transkeians who were
indicted shortly before independence, under the Suppression
of Communism Act, for allegedly setting up Marxist study
groups in Transkei between January 1974 and June 1976.
When the five appeared in court in Umtata in March, their
advocate, international law expert Professor John Dugard,
argued in vain that the case should be discharged as the
courts of one country could not punish offenses committed
against another state. This was countered successfully by the
Transkei attorney general, G. Titterton, who observed that
under clause 54(1)(c) of the Transkei Constitution his office
had discretion to continue with all cases pending at the time of
independence "as if Transkei had not become independent."
Obviously in this instance a political judgment had been made
to do just that.

In April an event occurred which suggested that the limits
of acceptable political dissent had narrowed even more. Pascoe
Ludidi, erstwhile chief whip of the government in the National
Assembly and TNIP general secretary at the time of the 1976
elections, crossed into Lesotho with his family on the eleventh
and asked for political asylum. A month earlier he had left
TNIP and joined the opposition in the National Assembly,
concurrently announcing the formation of the Transkei
United party. Thereafter, he said, "Radio Transkei as well as
Radio Bantu never broadcast any contribution I made in Parliament." At a press conference at Maseru, the Lesotho capital, Ludidi explained that he had fled to Lesotho because the
Transkei authorities were "trying to isolate me from public
opinion with a view to suppressing me or . . . before detaining
me" (4/15).

For more than seven months after independence, all the South African security legislation that applied in Transkei before October 26, 1976, continued to apply. This included the Suppression of Communism Act, the Unlawful Organizations Act, the Riotous Assemblies Act, and the Internal Security Act, among others, not to mention Proclamation R400. Yet, however convenient the powers provided under these statutes from the government's point of view, their liability from a public relations perspective could not be doubted, since much of the world regards these laws as the handmaidens of apartheid. It was thus not surprising when President Botha Sigcau revealed, when opening the National Assembly on March 9, that the government planned to introduce its own security legislation. However, the suggested terms of the proposed bill, which the prime minister had touched upon a fortnight earlier, prompted immediate alarm. Matanzima indicated that his government wanted to make it a treasonable offense, retroactive to October 26, 1976, and punishable by death, to cast doubt on Transkei sovereignty or to suggest that "Transkei should fall under another independent state." President Sigcau did not mention the feature of retroactivity, but he added that "office bearers of the State" would be similarly protected against efforts to discredit them. [3]

When the Public Security Bill finally appeared on May 13, it proved to be an omnibus measure which, though repealing all of the South African laws cited above (and Proclamation R400), in fact incorporated their principal features into Transkeian law. The proposed act, which passed the assembly on the last day of the session, empowered the Transkei minister of justice, acting free of review by any court or authority, to

1. outlaw particular organizations;
2. impose restrictions on persons who have been members or active supporters of outlawed organizations;
3. proscribe meetings of more than ten persons;
4. restrict named individuals from leaving a particular area or from attending a designated gathering; or
5. detain persons without charge.

3. Ibid., p. 2.

Additionally the bill proscribed acts or statements "which subvert, or are intended to subvert, the authority of the State and its officers." And as the prime minister had forewarned, the legislation defined the propagation of the view that "Transkei, or parts of Transkei, should form another country, or part of a country" as treason, for conviction of which the death sentence could be imposed. (Because of this provision the Democratic party soon found it advisable to delete from its own constitution a clause declaring Transkei to be an "integral part" of South Africa [8/27]). The idea of retroactive application of the law had been dropped, however.

One feature of the Public Security Bill as first published that the government agreed to eliminate later was a clause outlawing all organizations banned in South Africa. The opposition in the National Assembly recognized immediately that this would include the African National Congress and the Pan-Africanist Congress. Matanzima's relations with both these organizations have been ambiguous at best, but at independence he did promise to allow both bodies to continue their "liberation struggle" against South Africa from Transkei territory as long as they did not use Transkei to wage an *armed* struggle against its neighbor. Indeed, in March 1976 Matanzima publicly promised to ask South Africa, after independence, to return to Transkei all Xhosa-speaking prisoners held on Robben Island, which would include, among others, Matanzima's distant relative Nelson Mandela, leader of the ANC. And, at independence, the prime minister appointed a one-time PAC political exile, Tsepo T. Letlaka, to the post of minister of finance.

Also in May the government brought forward legislation establishing the Transkei Intelligence Service (TIS) under the control of the prime minister, with responsibility for intelligence and security-related activities that are undertaken in the republic by the Bureau for State Security. The 1977–78 budget estimates showed a grant of $579,000 for this purpose. A Publications Bill introduced in the National Assembly provided for the official censorship of literature, films, and public entertainment. Early in August a police raid on a bookshop in the prestigious Holiday Inn in Umtata showed an official concern with pornographic rather than political materials, but in context it seemed inevitable that the new Publications Control Board would become a partisan ally of the government. Indeed, a few days later the commissioner for Inland Revenue, M. W. Pretorius, said in Umtata that all books that were banned in South Africa before independence (including a great many on political grounds) remained banned in Transkei (8/9). In May, too, the government introduced legislation in the National Assembly requiring newspapers published in Transkei to be registered. The bill required newspaper proprietors, at the time of registration, to deposit up to $23,000 with the government, which could be forfeited if the paper published "undesirable material." Minister of the Interior Stella Sigcau explained that the bill would enable the government to keep a check on "subversive activities."[4]

On June 7, 1976, in a speech in the House of Assembly previously cited in chapter 3, Colin Eglin, leader of the Progressive Reform party (as it was then named), listed three conditions which, if met, would allow his party to support Transkei independence. This was an important speech in that it set out the bare minimum requirements of a tolerable separatism from an essentially liberal point of view. The first condition, mentioned earlier, was that Transkei independence should "be tested by an open referendum." The second condition was that no South African citizen should be compelled to become a citizen of Transkei against his will. (Eglin is unclear here whether he is referring to the urban Xhosa outside Transkei, or perhaps even to Transkei residents as well.) And the third condition, which is relevant here, is that the Transkei Constitution should include a bill of rights safeguarding minorities and the basic rights of all citizens.[5] At the end of the first year of Transkei independence, it was clear that the civil liberties of its citizens were not being scrupulously protected in the new state, but in private, at least, this conclusion appeared less troubling to some African nationalists than to most white liberals. A prominent black political figure in

4. Ibid., p. 416.
5. *House of Assembly Debates,* June 7, 1976, cols. 8369–72.

Botswana with close connection to Transkei, for example, is reported to have said recently:

> I am not bothered by the absence of freedom in Transkei. I can understand that Kaiser would want to stop dissent at this stage. After all, Africa is not very democratic. How long did it take the U.S.A. to become democratic?[6]

Parties

In 1964–65, when I wrote the chapter on the "first year" of self-government for *South Africa's Transkei,* the emergence of political parties in the territory was an obvious and necessary theme. Now, a dozen years later, the virtual elimination of competitive party politics from Transkei is the point that must be emphasized. The ruling TNIP, of course, survives, but as a rusty political machine little pressed by its nominal opposition, which are parties in name only. The radical Democratic party of Hector Ncokazi, which showed promise of developing broad appeal, was effectively suppressed by police detentions of its executive at the time of the 1976 elections, as mentioned earlier, and while the DP fielded eleven candidates anyway (though some were still in jail), only one of these was returned. (That one, however, P. N. Nkosiyane, soundly beat the long-time leader of the opposition, Knowledge Guzana, at Mqanduli.) At the end of the year the only DP executive member not still being detained, J. Kobo, announced that the party would dissociate itself from the affairs of the National Assembly in Umtata and instead focus its attentions on Transkeians in the cities (12/10). Still, Ncokazi remained in jail. In late April it was reported that Ncokazi, now released, had spent a total of 212 days in detention since his arrest the preceding July (4/29).

Until January 1976 the head of the Democratic party had been Knowledge Guzana, who was clearly the best-known resident Transkeian abroad, apart from Kaiser Matanzima himself, and the one most admired. But at that time, following several earlier attempts, Guzana was finally dislodged from the DP leadership by Ncokazi, who immediately substi-

6. Confidential source.

tuted the ideology of "black consciousness" for the party's traditional policy of liberal "multiracialism." Guzana then withdrew from the party he had helped to found in 1964, and in April he formed the New Democratic party, which despite its name became the clear ideological successor to the Democratic party of Paramount Chief Victor Poto in the late 1960s. With seven of twelve opposition seats in the last TLA, Guzana held on to his position as leader of the opposition, and in the 1976 elections his party entered sixteen candidates. But only two of these were elected, and lacking thereafter the leadership that had been provided by the sophisticated and experienced Guzana, the New Democratic party similarly became dormant in the National Assembly.

On October 15, 1976, when the results of the recent elections were made public, Matanzima was asked whether, with just seven opposition members in the National Assembly (three of whom were ex-officio chiefs), he was considering making Transkei a one-party state. His response was that while he was opposed to outlawing opposition groups, he expected that the MPs still outside TNIP would soon decide voluntarily to join it (10/16). Indeed, at the outset of the new National Assembly an independent, Harold Zibi, did cross to the government saying, "I had been strongly opposed to the amputation of Transkei from South Africa and the policy of separate development, but these are now of the past." But at the same time the irrepressible Cromwell Diko, who had been elected as a TNIP member, crossed from the government and announced the founding of the Transkei People's Freedom party. With the support of three other members, all former supporters of the Democratic party, Diko was designated leader of the opposition. In this position he was frequently quoted in the press, but a surer sign of his importance occurred in March, when the first annual congress of the Transkei People's Freedom party in Umtata had to be called off because only three persons showed up (3/7).

Relations with South Africa
As the most common criticism of Transkei independence is that the territory cannot, by reason of its circumstances, be independent of South Africa, it seemed probable on October

26 that the new government would seek an early opportunity
to demonstrate that it could act independently, and that a
striving for independence would be a recognizable theme of
the new administration. During the first year such an effort
was in fact made, including domestic changes designed to
assert a distinctive Transkei identity, such as the announcement in June that all road signs in Afrikaans would be removed and that only signs in either English or Xhosa would
be permitted. Here Transkei's direct relations with Pretoria
will be discussed, the character of which, Gwendolen Carter
has predicted, "is likely to have considerable influence on external, and even internal, attitudes towards the territory."[7]

The independence celebrations themselves were notable
for the spirit of harmony and good will that prevailed between representatives of the two states and that was manifest
by the Transkei public in Umtata toward the republican officials who were present, including State President Nico Diederichs. This spirit appears to have characterized the state
visit of Prime Minister and Mrs. Vorster to Umtata for two
days in January. Yet less than three weeks after independence,
a step in a different spirit was taken that was presumably intended to be highly symbolic (and was, in fact, reminiscent
of generally similar steps taken by a number of newly independent African governments earlier, in West and Equatorial
Africa). Without apparent warning to Pretoria, the Transkei
cabinet ordered all South African policemen (eighteen in
number) to leave the territory "forthwith" (11/12). A less
dramatic news story appearing some days before conveyed a
contrary image, however. On October 29 the *Daily Dispatch*
reported that the South African Railways administration
would continue, as before, to operate rail and some bus service in Transkei and maintain lighthouses along the Transkei
coast.

The budget address by the minister of finance, T. T. Letlaka,
on March 23, was another sobering reminder of Transkei's
overwhelming dependence on Pretoria. For notwithstanding
unprecedented new taxes on the peasantry (for example,
a livestock tax of $11.50 per head of cattle, and an increase

7. Gwendolen M. Carter and Patrick O'Meara, eds., *Southern Africa in
Crisis* (Bloomington: Indiana University Press, 1977), p. 116.

in the hut tax by 1,000 percent), later scaled down by half, in order to reduce (in the minister's words) the "massive shortfall between revenue and expenditure," the government revealed that it relied on assistance from Pretoria to cover 58 percent of just current expenditures for 1977–78.[8] In September the *Daily Dispatch* reported that the Matanzima cabinet was considering ways of reducing the state's dependence on foreign governments and increasing Transkei's self-sufficiency (9/22). But apparently these did not include a drastic curtailment of the costs of government; at $273 million the 1977–78 Transkei budget was 75 percent larger than the one for the preceding year. Much of this increase was clearly a result of a striking growth in the size of Transkei's civil service. From December 1975 to December 1976, 5,766 positions were added to the "fixed establishment," representing an increase in one year of nearly 50 percent.[9]

Press accounts reveal three other foci of concern in relations between Umtata and Pretoria during the former's first year of independence: (1) the definition of who in the republic are Transkei citizens, (2) how Transkei citizens are treated in the republic, and (3) Transkei land claims. Each of these topics will be treated separately.

Citizenship. Pretoria's strategy at independence appeared to be to reassure the urban Xhosa that they would not suffer in consequence of Transkei's changed status and that for the moment nothing extraordinary was expected of them, while concurrently not relinquishing the key principle that these individuals had *in law* ceased to be South African citizens and were now Transkei nationals. Against the background of four months of the most widespread and protracted rioting by urban Africans (and in Cape Town, coloureds) in South Africa's history, this caution was understandable. In a radio broadcast on October 24, Minister M. C. Botha declared that Transkei citizens living in the republic "would not lose any existing rights, privileges or benefits" (10/25/76). And two days later, independence day, *The Star* quoted F. B. du Randt,

8. *Debates of the National Assembly, 1977*, pp. 67–70.
9. Transkei Government, *Annual Report of the Public Service Commission, 1976*, p. 3.

chief Bantu Affairs commissioner for the Witwatersrand,
who gave these details of the policy:

Any Transkei citizen who is legally in any area of South
Africa at the moment remains unhindered wherever he is.
He does not have to get any additional documentation, he
remains in possession of his reference book and in fact
may even change work within the Republic without having
to return to Transkei. At the end of a two year interim
period these Transkei citizens will have to get a Transkei
identity document. That is all.

Pretoria thus hoped to put off repercussions of the change for
two years.

Yet, almost immediately, lower-echelon white officials
confounded this timetable. In early January Transkei's ambassador to South Africa, Professor M. Njisane, decried instances
in which Xhosa speakers born outside Transkei had been refused South African documents and told they would have to
apply for Transkei passports (1/7). The Transkei consulate in
Cape Town reported similar cases. High-level discussions on
the issue ensued, but with no discernible result. Then, in early
August, the republican government's decision to evict many
thousands of African squatters from their shantytowns on
the Cape flats, and thereafter to demolish the structures
themselves, raised the question to crisis proportions, for most
of the dispossessed were Xhosa speakers, and Pretoria's announced intention was that those lacking permission to be in
the peninsula region would be repatriated to either Transkei
or the Ciskei. But during an urgent visit to Cape Town, the
Transkei foreign minister, Digby Koyana, declared his country would not, and could not, accept all the Xhosa people the
South African government might try to send it. "They are
South Africa's responsibility," Koyana said. "If there has to
be a confrontation about this, then there will simply have to
be a confrontation." The foreign minister openly wondered
if there was any justification for continued diplomatic ties
between Umtata and Pretoria (8/10).

These statements would appear to have contributed to the
visit to Umtata at the end of the month of the South African
foreign minister, Pik Botha, and his senior cabinet colleague,

Dr. Connie Mulder, minister of interior. Yet in early September so disgusted was Ambassador Njisane by continued police raids near Cape Town on groups of squatters, who had now retreated to church properties opened to them by the local congregations, that he announced to the press he "would gladly close his office and return to Transkei if told to do so by his Prime Minister" (9/10).

The matter of the Cape Town squatters was understandably high on the agenda of the talks that took place between Matanzima and Vorster in Pretoria later in September, during the former's first state visit to South Africa. These talks were subsequently chracterized by the Transkei prime minister as "frank, straightforward, and brutal at times" (9/17). But they appear also to have been fruitful. Two weeks later negotiations on the specific issue commenced between the two governments at ambassadorial level, and a week after this, a provisional agreement was announced. Transkei accepted South Africa's desire to stop illegal squatting, and South Africa agreed to stay further immediate action against the peninsula squatters while the two governments worked together to deal with the situation (10/8). The issue of Transkei citizenship thus appeared to have been successfully deferred.

Treatment of Transkei citizens in South Africa. Intertwined in August with the question of whether South Africa could unilaterally declare many of the peninsula squatters Transkei citizens and repatriate them to Transkei was the issue of the treatment accorded persons in South Africa whom Transkei acknowledged to be its citizens. Umtata's view was put succinctly by Foreign Minister Koyana in Cape Town on August 9: "We completely reject the concept that our citizens should be treated any differently to aliens from any other independent country" (8/10). Yet in February the Pretoria government made it clear that (in the words of a newspaper report) there would be "no honorary white status" for Transkeians in South Africa. On February 14, V. Schoeman, deputy secretary for the Department of Community Development, put the policy as follows: "There is no difference in the position of Transkeians and persons from Soweto.

It cannot possibly be otherwise" (2/15). And a month later South African Foreign Minister Hilgard Muller (who was shortly to retire) admitted in parliament that while the government was "giving attention to this," Transkeians remained subject to pass laws and influx control regulations while in the republic (3/16). The legal basis for this view appears to be an agreement between the governments of Transkei and South Africa signed just before independence, in which it is stated that Transkeians obtaining employment in South Africa shall do so "subject to the prevailing laws of the Republic" (2/19).

For nearly all Transkeians, therefore, the ending of apartheid was limited to the territory itself. The exceptions were the very few Transkeians in South Africa in official roles. An illustration of these exceptions (which were particularly newsworthy, although black diplomats from Malawi and the United States had been accommodated in South Africa for some years previous) was contained in a report on October 7, 1977, in *Indaba,* the weekly supplement of the *Daily Dispatch* and the *Eastern Province Herald* (Port Elizabeth) intended for Xhosa-speaking readers. *Indaba* printed three pictures of the Transkei consul's residence in Durban (Umhlanga) and a story giving its cost as $75,000. Earlier, the price paid for the Johannesburg consul's home in the exclusive Houghton suburb was said to be $219,000. Yet even Transkei officials were periodically embarrassed in South Africa, as African diplomats in the United States were sometimes victims of local race discrimination as late as the 1960s. In March the deputy secretary of the Transkei Department of Information was refused service at the fashionable Kennaway Hotel in East London. And even Prime Minister Matanzima is reported to have experienced some momentary difficulty being served in a restaurant in Queenstown in July. The white proprietor of the Anglo Cafe explained to newsmen, "I have to abide by the law of the country. It did not matter whether they were from the independent Transkei" (7/22).

Land. In chapter 3 it was seen that Transkeian claims for additional land from white South Africa blocked moves toward independence for the territory for some years, and that this impediment was removed only in 1974 when Matanzima appeared to accept that boundary adjustments with the republic could be made after independence as readily as before. In 1975 two new magisterial districts (Herschel and Glen Grey) and their respective populations were added to the twenty-six districts that had previously made up Transkei, but these two had formerly been part of the Ciskei homeland and were not white lands at all. (These additions were approved by the Ciskei government, which received in turn some neighboring white lands from Pretoria, although four years earlier a large majority of African voters in the Glen Grey district [85.1 percent] voting in a referendum on the issue had rejected incorporation into Transkei. At independence there were reports of thousands of Africans fleeing these two districts back into South Africa in order to avoid Transkei citizenship.) In his Independence Day speech, Matanzima pointedly declined to accept Transkei's boundaries as "final." It will be remembered that the lands openly coveted by Umtata, in addition to the internal "white spots," all of which became part of Transkei on or before October 26, consisted of four magisterial districts to the territory's north and west, Matatiele, Mount Currie, Elliot, and Maclear. Journalists at the prime minister's press conference on the second day of independence were thus surprised when he ignored these areas and, instead, articulated ambitions to incorporate the Ciskei, or as later clarified, lands in but not of the Ciskei. The excited headline in the *Daily Dispatch* on October 28 read, "Kaiser: I Will Take Ciskei." This idea of a unilateral incorporation of Ciskei lands was soon replaced by the more diplomatic suggestion that the Ciskei and Transkei should join together to make one Xhosa nation (1/26), although it reappeared in late March in the form of a unanimous motion of the National Assembly.[10] Meanwhile, however, Matanzima refocused his territorial ambitions on lands to the west and north, and from early March these areas, rather than the Ciskei, were again central to press reports from Umtata.

10. *Debates of the National Assembly, 1977,* p. 87.

The timing of Matanzima's renewed interest in these areas was probably influenced by the appointment of the so-called Steyn Committee by the Cape and Natal provincial administrations to consider the future of those areas of the Cape Province that were now separated by Transkei territory from the rest of the province. Known as East Griqualand, these areas included the lands claimed by Transkei in the Matatiele and Mount Currie districts. The popular expectation was that the Steyn Committee would recommend that these districts should now be joined to Natal. Two days before a republican minister indicated that the Steyn Committee had submitted its report to the two provincial administrators, Matanzima threatened an "armed struggle" if his land demands were not met, in a speech in Umtata opening the annual TNIP congress. But this time Matanzima claimed not only the districts previously mentioned but also lands in Natal west of the Umzimkulu River, which appeared to put him into direct conflict with KwaZulu (and Chief Buthelezi) as well as with Pretoria (3/9). Ten days after this, Foreign Minister Hilgard Muller announced in parliament that his government "differs fundamentally from the Transkeian Government with respect to the matter [of land] and can therefore not support its assertion" (3/19). But Matanzima persisted. Speaking in the National Assembly on April 22, he said Transkei would "act immediately" should East Griqualand be officially incorporated into Natal. "We know what steps we shall take and all I can say now is that we shall await the bill that will be published in the South African parliament declaring this portion of Transkeian territory as Natal."[11] (Much later Foreign Minister Pik Botha would say in parliament in Cape Town that he had learned in private conversations with the Transkei prime minister that Matanzima's fear was that if land claimed by Transkei was given to Natal, it would end up in KwaZulu [6/14].) Undaunted, the administrator of the Cape, Dr. L. Munnik, said in Cape Town on May 17 that the government and the Steyn Committee had officially rejected Transkei's claims to East Griqualand and had decided that the territory should be ceded to Natal (5/18); the cession was later sched-

11. Ibid., p. 239.

uled to occur on April 1, 1978. Matanzima was thus given a breathing space of more than ten months to consider his response.

Relations with other states
The central issue during the first year of independence was Transkei's search for international recognition. This interest was not grounded so much in material as in symbolic considerations, although Transkei would probably qualify for foreign assistance from such developed countries as recognized it. For recognition was intimately linked with the perceived legitimacy of the new state, and until such time as some countries other than South Africa recognized Transkei, there was a sense in which, for its own people, its independence was not yet real, or fully established.

Eleven months before independence it was clear that recognition was going to be a problem for Transkei. On November 28, 1975, the UN General Assembly resolved (Res. 3411 D [XXX]) by 99 votes to 0, with 8 abstentions, to block recognition of Transkei or of any other Bantustan. The relevant clause here is the last one, but I will quote all three in order to convey more fully the sentiment of the General Assembly toward Transkei independence.

> The General Assembly, . . .
> *Taking note* of the manoeuvres of the racist regime of South Africa to proceed with the establishment of bantustans in the Transkei and other regions;
> *Reaffirming* the legitimacy of the struggle of the South African people, under the leadership of their national liberation movements, by all means possible, for the total eradication of apartheid and for the exercise of their right to self-determination;
> 1. *Again condemns* the establishment of bantustans as designed to consolidate the inhuman policies of apartheid, to perpetuate white minority domination and to dispossess the African people of South Africa of their inalienable right to their country;
> 2. *Reaffirms* that the establishment of bantustans is a measure essentially designed to destroy the territorial

integrity of the country in violation of the principles enshrined in the Charter of the United Nations;

3. *Calls upon* all Governments and organizations not to
deal with any institutions or authorities of the bantustans
or to accord any form of recognition to them. [12]

The eight countries that abstained on this vote included
most of South Africa's major trading partners, especially
France, West Germany, the United Kingdom, and the U.S.A.,
but as these states also have substantial interests in black
Africa, it seemed likely that they too would be guided in
their attitudes toward Transkei by the majority, since it included most of the members of the Organization of African
Unity. And to ensure that Africa remained united on this
issue, the Council of Ministers of the OAU decided on June 28,
1976, to make it compulsory for all its members to refuse to
recognize the new state. There was thus a note of anticlimax
to the announcement at the end of September that the nine
European Common Market countries had decided against
recognition. [13]

Although the House of Representatives in Washington resolved against extending U.S. recognition to Transkei on September 21, 1976, the official American position was left ob-
scure until independence day itself, possibly in order not to
confuse Secretary Kissinger's concurrent efforts to mediate
(with South Africa's help) the Rhodesian dispute. Indeed, in
September and October there was some speculation (even on
the floor of the House of Representatives) that America might
barter U.S. recognition of Transkei for South African concessions on Rhodesia or perhaps Namibia. But on October 26
the Department of State issued the following statement:

We have indicated that we do not intend to recognize the
Transkei as an independent state. With regard to the homelands as presently constituted, [they] cannot be regarded
as a just division of South Africa's territory. In expressing

12. General Assembly, *Resolutions Adopted by the General Assembly during Its Thirtieth Session, 16 September–17 December 1975*
(New York: United Nations, 1976), p. 37.

13. *Rand Daily Mail*, June 29, 1976; *Pretoria News*, September 28,
1976.

this judgment we have been careful to emphasize that it is not for us to prescribe the solution the people of South Africa adopt to resolve their complex problems. However, we do believe that any such solution to be viable as well as just, must take into account the interests of all South Africans.[14]

Still, in the weeks just before October 26, it was widely expected that at least some of the world's lesser (and right-wing) states would send representatives to Umtata on independence day, implying an international recognition of sorts. The names of the countries often suggested were Taiwan, Rhodesia, Malawi, and Uruguay. But in fact the thirty or so parliamentarians from Europe and South America and the one Uruguayan general who journeyed to Umtata were all there in unofficial capacities. Offically, Transkei independence was witnessed only by representatives of the two separating countries, and the absence of any other emissaries was a constant reminder of prevailing international opinion regarding the step.

On the other side of the world, however, the event prompted anti-South African demonstrations in a number of North American cities and (over Western objections) appearances before the UN General Assembly in New York by Oliver Tambo, acting-president of the African National Congress of South Africa, and David Sibeko, foreign affairs director for the Pan Africanist Congress. Following their speeches, 134 members of the General Assembly voted to declare Transkei independence "invalid" and to request member governments "to prohibit all individuals, corporations and other institutions from having any dealings with either the Transkei or any other future bantustan."[15] No state opposed this resolution and only the United States abstained. (The next day in Hartford, Connecticut, Secretary Kissinger explained that America had objected to the resolution on "technical" rather than substantive grounds, namely, that to prohibit dealings with the Transkei government was to

14. Quoted in the *Daily Dispatch,* September 18, 1977, source unknown.
15. *New York Times,* October 27, 1976.

acknowledge its existence, which America did not wish to do.)[16] For the new Republic of Transkei it was an inauspicious beginning, but a beginning nonetheless.

In early April it appeared that Ecuador might be the first state other than South Africa to recognize Transkei, when a nine-member delegation from that South American country arrived in Umtata for a four-day visit. Headed by a vice admiral, purportedly representing the president of Ecuador, the delegation also included a cabinet minister and the governor of the port city of Guayaquil. At the end of their stay the leader of the delegation spoke of the "nobleness" of Transkei and invited Prime Minister Matanzima to make a return visit to Ecuador. This invitation was immediately accepted (4/5). But five weeks later the Foreign Ministry in Ecuador denied that any official mission had been in the region and indicated the country's intention to uphold the General Assembly's resolution "concerning the case of the so-called independent Transkei." Transkeian Foreign Minister Koyana, obviously disappointed, speculated that the Ecuador government had "buckled" under foreign pressures that had arisen as a result of the delegation's visit to Umtata (5/11).

The practical consequences of nonrecognition concerned the freedom of Transkeians to travel abroad on Transkei passports and the related issue of representation of the new state throughout the world. Shortly after independence, spokesmen for Great Britain and the United States indicated that persons traveling on Transkei passports would not be allowed to enter those countries, save for humanitarian reasons; and in time it was established that except for Switzerland, most European countries had taken a similar position, at least initially. At Christmastime a woman carrying a Transkei passport was in fact refused entry into Botswana (1/7). Yet, throughout the year, periodic press accounts showed that some few Transkeians were succeeding in traveling overseas where travel had been thought impossible. Early in April the Transkei government declined to say what passports the minister of planning and commerce, Ramsay Madikizela, and his departmental secretary had used during a recent European

16. Department of State, *Bulletin*, November 22, 1976, p. 642.

trip (4/2), suggesting perhaps that they had traveled on South African documents. (The preceding November the Transkei secretary for foreign affairs, M. Lujabe, had anticipated this possibility [11/6].) But in June a member of the cast of the South African musical play *Umabatha* was permitted to enter Britain on a Transkei passport, prompting immediate criticism of the Home Office by the Anti-Apartheid Movement in Britain (6/15). And in August it was revealed that M. Leslie Masinimi, who was identified as Transkei's minister-at-large for North, Central, and South America, had spent some months in Washington, D.C., where his legal status was that of "permanent resident." The 1977 visits by official Transkei delegations in May to Taiwan and in October to Rhodesia were, of course, less surprising.

The Transkei government thus attempted to compensate for the absence of embassies abroad (except of course in Pretoria) with ad hoc visits by high-ranking officials to those governments that would receive them. Indeed, anticipating such visits, at independence Matanzima appointed a former cabinet minister, Chief Jeremiah Moshesh, a roving ambassador for Transkei. A different, though not incompatible, tactic that was followed in the cases of Britain and the United States involved hiring nationals of these countries to represent Transkei in their own capitals as "registered foreign agents." In America this individual, after March, was Jay Parker, a black public relations specialist, who succeeded another black American, Andrew Hatcher, a one-time assistant press secretary in the White House under President John F. Kennedy. In April Parker's monthly fee was reported to be $10,300, not including expenses (4/7). Transkei's representative in London was a West Indian, Scobie Loblack, a partner in a local public relations firm. "My job," Loblack said in August, "is to explain to Britain and Europe that Transkei is not a homeland. Neither is it some place ridden with mud huts and shacks. It has one of the highest literacy rates in Africa" (8/26).

Notwithstanding these arrangements, one's overriding impression of Transkei's international position during 1977 is of a country under involuntary quarantine. Thus, more important than the newspaper account of Transkei's admission in April as the first black African member of the Tug-of-War International Federation (whose headquarters are in neutral Switzerland), was the report two days earlier that the general secretary of the Nairobi-based All African Conference of Churches had turned down an invitation to visit Umtata. In his reply Canon Burgess Carr said it was "altogether impossible for me to appear to sanction the South African policy of Bantustans by visiting Transkei" (5/18). Understandably, this quarantine, though it had largely been expected, frustrated the Umtata government and resulted in periodic public statements of outrage. For example, four days after independence Matanzima reacted to the General Assembly's resolution cited earlier by calling the UN "a noisy conglomeration of . . . bloodthirsty people" and observing that it appeared that a new state had to be born violently in order for the world body to recognize it (10/30). And a month later Finance Minister Letlaka accused the West of bolstering apartheid by continuing to invest in South Africa while choosing to ignore Transkei (11/27). Again, in March, Matanzima bitterly noted in a speech in the National Assembly that

> today the British Government and all its henchmen pretend to be protectors of the black people in South Africa, while they recognize the sovereignty of the minority of Whites over the blacks in this country and while they are trading partners with South Africa.

But, appealing to history, the prime minister asked:

> What part did this great Empire play when the black people under Clements Kadalie were mercilessly killed in East London in 1928 when the ICU resolved against white domination? What part did the British Government play when the Africans of this colony—the Cape Province—were removed from the common roll as voters in 1936?[17]

Finally, on the first anniversary of independence, Matanzima entreated the United States directly, as the only country that had not supported the General Assembly's resolution on

17. *Debates of the National Assembly, 1977*, p. 26.

Transkei a year earlier, to reconsider its policy of nonrecognition.[18] The effort seemed to reveal both Matanzima's ignorance of the reason for the American abstention in 1976 and the overall desperation of the Umtata government's isolated position.

There was one substantive issue of international relations apart from dealings with South Africa that needs to be mentioned. No sooner had the General Assembly, on October 26, reiterated its opposition to recognition of Transkei than the territory's northwestern neighbor, Lesotho, charged that Transkei had closed their common border in order to try to force Lesotho to deal with the Umtata government. Lesotho's ambassador to the UN, Mooki Molapo, declared that his country was being victimized for upholding the will of the General Assembly, and he appealed for help. Foreign Minister Koyana denied this allegation, although conceding that Lesotho citizens wishing to enter Transkei required valid travel documents. "It follows," Koyana said, "that for people to be able to comply with these requirements they must acknowledge the sovereignty of Transkei" (11/10). But in New York on November 22 the Security Council condemned any action serving to force Lesotho into recognizing Transkei and appealed to all states to provide immediate aid to Lesotho (11/23). Ambassador Molapo said that $69 million was needed to open up the mountainous southeastern region of his country, which had been isolated by the dispute. At Christmas Koyana characterized Lesotho's efforts as an original fund-raising drive and added, "Good luck to them—they are doing quite well" (12/24).

At New Year's it was announced that the UN secretary-general intended sending a team of investigators to study the situation firsthand at the Lesotho-Transkei border. But before the UN mission arrived, in late January, the respected assistant editor of the London *Observer,* Colin Legum, visited the scene to make his own investigation; and later he wrote that the border was in fact open and that the UN had been "hoaxed" by the government of Lesotho into promising substantial relief aid (1/17). The UN mission visited Lesotho anyway, and a brief press account four months later indi-

18. *The Citizen,* October 27, 1977.

cated that the Security Council considered the mission's report on May 24. But with the Legum account, world interest in Lesotho's claims waned, and the issue soon died away.[19]

Economic development

Although Port St. Johns hoteliers complained in July, normally their high season, that (white) tourism to their region had fallen off sharply after independence due to "grossly exaggerated scare stories," overall the pattern of economic advance that was apparent before independence continued thereafter and indeed accelerated somewhat. At the end of January the TDC chairman, Franko Maritz, told the American Businessmen's Club in Johannesburg that whereas the TDC had concluded agreements with seven industrialists during the year just before independence, in only two months after independence nineteen agreements had been signed (2/1). Throughout the year periodic news stories told of the establishment of new factories, mainly in the Butterworth area—a wheat mill in November; a plant for the manufacture of automobile exhaust systems in February; a factory for the fabrication of structural steel for commercial vehicles, also in February; a food-processing plant in June, and so forth. Generally these factories appeared to be small-scale, involving capital investments of between $1 and $3 million and ultimately employing 100 to 200 Africans in each case. Yet compared with the totally bleak industrial picture in Transkei only a few years before, the cumulative impact of these individually small changes was impressive in this relative sense.

In September, however, an international development expert invited to Transkei, Professor J. D. Ben-Dak from the universities of Haifa and Vermont, properly noted that the development of Transkei was proceeding independently of any officially sanctioned development plan, indeed independently of any serious planning at all (9/22). Since June 1976

19. For additional details of the episode, see Theo Malan, "The Lesotho-Transkei Border Closure: Fact or Fallacy?" *Africa Institute Bulletin* 15, nos. 1 and 2 (1977): 36–39. A summary of the UN mission's report can be found in the periodical *Objective: Justice* (UN Office of Public Information) 9, no. 2 (September 1977): 22–37, under the title "Assistance to Lesotho: Report of the United Nations Mission to Lesotho."

the board of the Transkei Development Corporation has included five black Transkeians alongside five whites appointed by the Department of Bantu Administration in Pretoria, but the strategy followed by the TDC has continued to be substantially an opportunistic one. That is, emphasizing the attractions of cheap labor and tax concessions, the TDC has sought to encourage white industrialists to invest in Transkei with attention apparently being given only to the economic soundness of the proposition from the investor's point of view. The national needs of Transkei are assumed to be served if such individual investments increase the net employment opportunities in the territory. If these criteria are met, factories producing lollypop sticks (an actual case) are no less welcome than factories producing any other commodity. In particular, no consideration appears to have been given to the most desirable balance between agricultural and industrial expansion within overall Transkei development, although comparatively infrequent reports of the former appeared throughout the year. For example, in August the cabinet announced formation of a state tea corporation (8/16).

There is one element of Transkei's future economic development that was planned for in 1977, and by the government itself. In early June the Transkei cabinet considered and decided on the desirability of a free commercial port on the Indian Ocean. Subsequently, a French firm was signed to find the best location, for it had been accepted that silting at the mouth of the Mzimvubu River precluded the development of Port St. Johns for this purpose. In middle October Matanzima announced cabinet acceptance of a recommendation that the port be located at Mnganzana, twenty kilometers south of Port St. Johns, in an estuarine mangrove swamp (10/15). (Conservationists immediately objected.) The prime minister indicated that planning for the harbor would start soon, but he could not say where the capital for such an immense project would be found.

International reaction to the circumstances of Transkei's birth has fostered the widespread public opinion that Transkei is profoundly unlike other states, a case apart. It has been said several times earlier that on objective material grounds there are some other states in Africa and elsewhere with which Transkei compares favorably, although the number of such states is not great. Now it is observed that at the end of the first year of independence the politics of Transkei was similar to that of some other states in the so-called Third World. Overall, Transkei had become (or more accurately, had remained) a recognizable neomercantilist political system, to employ David Apter's typology of modernizing states. Structurally there was more pluralism than one would expect in a "mobilized" polity, though far less than in a liberal democracy ("reconciliation" system). Particularly in the economic field the Matanzima government appeared willing to give wide latitude for independent decision-making by management, especially the TDC. But in the overtly political field, although the National Assembly continued to function as an ostensibly independent body, the actual structure of state authority remained predominantly hierarchical, focused on the person of the prime minister. And as the theory of such neomercantilist systems anticipates, substantial (although still measured) amounts of coercion were employed to prevent, in Apter's words, "political cynicism [casting doubt] on the symbolic and sanctional aspects of authority."[20]

The position regarding political values (Apter's other main variable) confirms this characterization. Despite occasional references to Xhosa nationalism during the first year, the preoccupation of the Transkei state was with the maximization of instrumental, largely economic and administrative, goals. The ideal was not to restratify Transkei society, but rather to increase opportunity through the expansion of the economy and of the civil service, in short, to enlarge the existing "pyramid without changing the values associated with rank," to quote Apter again.[21] Ideology, particularly in the sense of a political religion, was notably absent. And while the prime minister seemed no less vain than leaders in many other parts of the continent, no cult of personality surrounded him; a doctrine of "Matanzima-ism" was unthinkable. Authority fol-

20. Apter, *Politics of Modernization*, pp. 408 ff., 413.
21. Ibid., p. 416.

lowed ritual patterns, although at the top it was exercised in
a materially grand style. Visitors to the territory reported
little excitement or sense of community purpose in the new
state.

Operationally there were some differences—certainly differences of emphasis—between the Transkei political system
during the first year of independence and the neomercantilist
"ideal type." As one would expect, leadership was personalized, decision-making was centralized, and the legislative role
was increasingly consultative. But the ruling party did not
appear to be well organized or strong, nor did party function-
aries emerge as an important interest group. Emphasis was
given to expanding education and acquiring functional and
technical skills, but Matanzima himself did not try to bridge
the gap between the traditional past and the modern present
and future. In particular, the government left it to the TDC
to plan the industrialization of the territory. Most of all,
Transkei was dependent (for jobs, financial aid, and technical
assistance) on outsiders to a degree without parallel elsewhere, a dependency that Transkei's leaders made no serious
effort to disguise or reduce.

Compared with its alternatives, the neomercantilist system
is alleged to be strong in its stability during periods of sus-
tained social change. Being more coercive, mobilization systems are less efficient technically and are subject to rapid
(and violent) variation in the area of political beliefs. Reconciliation systems, on the other hand, can lose efficiency and,
at times, legitimacy because of the need to accommodate
many divergent points of view. The neomercantilist system is
in effect a compromise between the need for political unity in
a context of multiple social loyalties and the need for information to aid in dealing successfully with complex issues.
Apter thus finds it the "optimal form of political system for
consolidation in countries in the early stages of modernization." But the inevitable requirement for political succession
challenges continuity in all polities, in neomercantilist systems probably more frequently than in reconciliation systems.
(Apter appears to concede this indirectly when he writes,
"For one thing, the presidential monarchy is a fairly stable

form of chief executive, at least during the time span of the first presidential monarch.")[22] The nuances of the Transkei case suggest that the succession of Matanzima (who is sixty-two years of age at this writing and is rumored to be in ill health) could result in appreciable political change within the territory.

This observation rests simply on the absence of some specific constraints on the selection of Transkei's second prime minister or on his policies thereafter. Ideology should not be a factor because none has been articulated outside perhaps of the small Democratic party. There are a few constant "verities" in Matanzima's pronouncements through the years, for example, a belief in the enduring value of chieftainship and support for "capitalism with a conscience." But overall, his government's policies have exhibited more pragmatism than political theory. One expects that the conservative Transkei population would resist a frontal attack on tribal structures, but tactful manipulation should be possible. No less a person than Paramount Chief Victor Poto of Western Pondoland advocated in 1963 the removal of ex-officio chiefs from the TLA to an upper house of chiefs with power only of legislative review, a suggestion that indeed more closely conformed to the traditional role of chiefs in Transkei than the position that did obtain.[23] And, of course, most of Transkei's capitalists, certainly the most powerful ones, are white aliens. In short, Transkei politics seem quite free of entrenched ideological commitments.

Existing political structures should prove no more burdensome. Formally, the prime minister is selected by the Transkei president from among the leaders of the majority party in the National Assembly, which is to say, the majority party decides. But as TNIP has never been seriously challenged since its founding in 1964 and its major personalities have all carried the burdens of ministerial office throughout this period, it is scarcely surprising that like the ruling parties in many African one-party, and one-party dominant, states it

22. Ibid., pp. 421, 411.
23. Carter, Karis, and Stultz, *South Africa's Transkei*, p. 134; Hammond-Tooke, *Command or Consensus*, p. 215.

has wasted away as an important political entity, or consent group.

Of the process here under discussion, Apter has written:

> The neomercantilist societies can become dynastic. A small group of people around a "presidential monarch" may become the equivalent of a royal lineage. They may choose incumbents of political office by very particularistic means.[24]

Apart from the possibility (which many observers discount) of the younger Matanzima succeeding his brother, this is likely the most promising suggestion: a small group of insiders could decide the succession according to *their* needs. But Kaiser Matanzima has so dominated Transkei politics since 1964 that it is difficult (especially at some distance) to estimate who the members of this inner circle might be, or what particularistic criteria would be relevant at the time. In passing, however, it perhaps should be noted here that a military coup against the Matanzima government would seem unlikely so long as white republican officers remain in several command positions or while Matanzima's son (2d Lt. Qaqambile Matanzima) is among the small number of black officers.

There is of course one constraint on the character of Transkei politics which is remorseless in its fixity: the territory's economic dependence on South Africa. It may not determine who will replace Matanzima, but it will certainly limit that individual's practical options thereafter. Yet it is clear that it is in Pretoria's interest that Transkei be perceived as fully independent politically; and it seems likely, therefore, that South Africa will studiously avoid intervening in Transkei's affairs, save in matters where South Africa's most vital interests are involved, and then as discreetly as possible. Moreover, while from the standpoint of Umtata there can be no foreseeable escape from the need to export labor to the republic, this labor is also a vital part of the South African economy. South Africa could scarcely close its doors to Transkei workers without hurting itself. With respect to Transkei's financial dependence on South Africa, Umtata has

24. Apter, *Politics of Modernization,* p. 410.

but one practical alternative. I exclude the possibility of accepting, as Lesotho has, a drastic reduction in the level of governmental services, which would seem politically unfeasible. That alternative is for Transkei to try to balance the aid it receives from South Africa with assistance from other countries. Yet for the moment this option is effectively blocked by the failure of Transkei to secure international recognition. The Transkei state is thus in the grip of a peculiar vicious circle. Its financial dependence on South Africa is seen by other countries in part as grounds for not recognizing Transkei, but nonrecognition prevents the development of alternative sources of assistance that could lessen that dependence.

From Pretoria's standpoint this situation is not without benefit, although clearly the white regime would prefer that Transkei receive some international recognition. Transkei's isolation and related dependence on Pretoria enhances South Africa's control of its own borders. Indeed, toward the end of 1977 it seemed that this relationship between the two states might soon be tested. It was reported from Botswana that some political exiles were debating whether an African-controlled Transkei might not hold for them some unexplored advantages in their ongoing struggle with the South African state.[25]

25. Confidential source.

6

THE MEANING OF
TRANSKEI INDEPENDENCE

Four previous chapters have presented relevant facts of the
Transkei "situation" as these have been suggested by issues
arising from the separatist perspective that is fundamental to
this work. Many of these facts have been drawn from primary
sources, but a larger number were collected in the first instance by others—scholars, newspaper reporters, compilers of
official reports, and the like. Given, therefore, the varied ori-
gins of this information, its internal consistency is impressive.
Troubling disagreements among presumed authorities concerning empirical questions are rare, and one notes that personalities and organizations as diverse as the S.A. Institute of
Race Relations, the minister of Bantu Administration and
Development, and the periodical *The African Communist*
have relied on much the same statistics. Moreover, while lacu-
nae within the corpus of available data are clearly present,
particularly at the microlevel of Transkei affairs, what is now
known with confidence would seem adequate to support
some overarching conclusions. The suggestion of high-level
official corruption requires corroboration. One wishes for
more detail concerning the true sentiments of the Transkei
peasantry than can be provided by elections in what is virtually a one-party context. And I have previously pointed to

the desirability of research on the sensitive relationship between the Transkei government and the management of the
Transkei Development Corporation, not to mention the small
but growing number of voluntary associations in the territory. However, these are tasks for the future and need not
delay the job of trying to assess the significance of Transkei
independence.

What, then, should be the overall judgment concerning
Transkei independence? Is it a legitimate step or a sham?
Does it contribute to fundamental change in the race relations of the region, or does it impede such change? Considering what others have already said about these and similar
questions, and as a corollary to the earlier point that the facts
concerning Transkei are seldom in dispute, I have been struck
by the importance of the conceptual frame, or perspective,
of the observer. How one conceptualizes this situation, it
seems, substantially predetermines one's conclusions. The
outcome of the analysis hinges on the premises of the analysis; change the premises and the conclusions change too. This
is true for the Pretoria regime and for the radicals as well.
The radical, or revolutionary, paradigm has been beyond the
concern of this present work, especially since its arguments
do not appear to turn on a differential appreciation of the
regime's Bantustan policy, or of Transkei independence in
particular.[1] However, it is the premise of this work that if
revolutionary change is not to occur in South Africa, some
other type of change must take place to relieve the present
grievances of the oppressed peoples; and the specific alternatives to revolution considered here have been referred to as
separatism. Transkei's independence will now be considered
in the light of several of these alternatives.

Partition
Under the general theme of separatism, this work has given
particular emphasis to the notion of a racial partition of
South Africa. The underlying premise of this approach is

1. For an examination of Transkei independence from this perspective, see *Sechaba* (official organ of the African National Congress in
exile) 10, no. 4 (1976): 1–5; and *The African Communist*, no. 69
(1977): 35–41.

clearly the belief that societies that are bitterly divided along ethnic, or (loosely) cultural, lines are likely to be unable to work out their political differences within the framework of a single state in a manner that is tolerably consistent with liberal principles and democratic government. Contemporary Northern Ireland, Lebanon, and pre-1947 India are often cited in apparent support of this view. The idea that "democracy is inapplicable within a united South Africa" is, of course, familiar as a National party defense of apartheid, and indeed that policy is frequently represented by its proponents as if it were synonymous with partition.[2] Yet if the definition of the meaning of partition is taken from the academic and other authorities cited in chapter 1, rather than from statements of the South African regime, it is obvious that the steps leading to Transkei independence fall far short of what a partition of South Africa would require, even if we limit our concern to the so-called Transkeian Xhosa.

The principal problem with Transkei independence is that it does not lessen the reality of white privilege and the political supremacy of whites within the region. Nor does it introduce a radical departure from past practice in the allocation of resources in southern Africa; economic dependency of Transkeian Africans on whites remains. Transkei independence has not increased the physical separation of the races, and in particular it has not removed the curse of race discrimination within white-claimed South Africa. In short, it does not cut deeply enough into the prior "stratification system of race relations," to quote Tiryakian.[3]

Transkei independence is not partition of South Africa because it is blatantly unfair to African interest, which implies that independence is unlikely to reduce African grievances, especially among the urban Xhosa, whose low levels of participation in Transkei elections reinforce this conclusion. Transkei independence does not constitute an *equitable* division of what I have called the "common South African estate" by any acceptable understanding of that word.

2. See, for example, Minister M. C. Botha's introduction of the Status of Transkei Bill, *House of Assembly Debates,* June 7, 1976, cols. 8307–08.

3. Tiryakian, "Sociological Realism," p. 218.

But what, it may be asked, would "fairness" or "equity" mean in such a case? Over the years critics have never tired of pointing out that under the laws of the republic enacted by a whites-only parliament, Africans, who in 1970 comprised about 70 percent of the total population, have been prevented from owning land except within the homelands, which together constituted less than 14 percent of the surface area of South Africa in 1976. At the same time, whites, who were just under 18 percent of the population in 1970, have laid exclusive claim to the remaining 86 percent of the country, minus the so-called group areas set aside for the coloureds and Asians. The unfairness of such an allocation is clear, but what would be a fair division? Would it require that Africans receive 70 percent of the territory? Incidentally, on this basis the de facto population of Transkei should be entitled to a territory 2.6 times larger than the present country. But what if the African 70 percent were to include all the least productive lands and the whites kept control of the mineral wealth of the Witwatersrand and all the major cities? The briefest consideration of this emotion-laden question demonstrates that no simple a priori formula will do.

In the end I am persuaded that the key consideration determining whether a particular partition plan will be accepted as "fair" is the decision-making process by which that plan is reached. To be broadly accepted as "fair" and "equitable," it seems evident that a partition agreement must result from a decision-making process characterized by (1) the fullest participation by authentic representation of all relevant groups, and (2) intense bargaining among those representatives with all parties negotiating from positions of strength. This is reminiscent of the "participation hypothesis," which holds that "significant changes in human behavior [in this instance a change in the focus of African political aspirations] can be brought about rapidly only if the persons who are expected to change participate in deciding what the change shall be and how it shall be made."[4] Clearly, this sort of decision-making did not precede Transkei independence. Apart from the fact that the key negotiations with Pretoria

4. Sidney Verba, *Small Groups and Political Behavior* (Princeton: Princeton University Press, 1961), p. 206.

were held in secret and included for Transkei only the two
Matanzima brothers, the principal deficiency is that thereafter no African could see that the whites of South Africa
had given up anything of substance in order that Transkei
independence should occur. On the contrary, it appeared that
the whites had *gained* greater respectability for their exclusion of blacks from equal treatment in the cities. Nor could it
be believed that the Transkei representatives enjoyed effective leverage in the negotiations themselves. Certainly Pretoria wished Transkei to seek independence in order to vali-
date its policy of separate development, but there is no
evidence that the Vorster government was made to pay a high
price to ensure its happening. In short, Transkei independence lacks the legitimizing element of real and material
sacrifices on the part of the white population. As we have
seen, the principal issue in this regard for Matanzima was the
matter of land. However, he was forced in the end to back
down on his 1972 threat to Vorster that he would never request independence for Transkei "if part of our land still
remains in the Republic."[5] Although political power has ex-
changed hands in consequence of Transkei independence, if
only the power Transkeians now have, in Adam's words, to
"police themselves and administer their own poverty," there
has been no shifting in the ownership of great amounts of
wealth.[6] Some few whites may have been materially dis-
advantaged by the change, principally the 10,000 or so
whites who lived within the territory, but their number compared with the total white population of the republic, or the
extent of their loss, has not been great.

Could Transkei independence not lead to a truer form of
partition? What if Transkei were to join with the neighboring
Ciskei, which is also Xhosa-speaking, and the intervening port
city, East London, and white farmlands were to be included?
Would not the resulting "Greater Xhosaland" be a far more
credible nation-state and thereby be more likely to elicit
broader African interest and support? Can we not conceive of

5. Laurence, *The Transkei,* p. 92.
6. Heribert Adam, "Three Perspectives on the Future of South
Africa," unpublished manuscript, typescript, p. 17.

Transkei independence as merely a first step toward an eventual federation of black states of southern Africa? The assumption, of course, is that a similar process of consolidation, expansion, and strengthening of the other homelands would occur concurrently, and that changes toward deracialization would be introduced in the white "homeland" as well. It is conceivable that the deficiencies of the current policy which Transkei independence now highlights may prompt a new round of thinking on the part of policymakers. In the past, official race policy has been future-oriented in the sense that it has anticipated the independence of the homelands, after which, many whites comfortably believed, the more undesirable aspects of race relations in South Africa would simply disappear. But Transkei is now independent and most of the former tensions remain, particularly in the urban areas of the republic. It seems possible that an awareness of this fact could feed back and assist in the formulation of a more sweeping partition. Indeed, a renewed discussion of partition in the South African press in the middle of 1977 suggested that this was already occurring.[7] And it might be thought that the government of an independent Transkei would have greater freedom of action than the government of a dependent Bantustan in securing concessions from Pretoria, although nothing in the first year of Transkei independence has provided evidence for this contention.

On the other hand there are five reasons why Transkei independence could lessen the chances for a truer partition of southern Africa. In the first place, there probably would be resistance to Transkei's becoming part of some larger political entity on the part of officeholders in Transkei who would lose status or power as a result of such a step. Independence creates vested interests that may be difficult subsequently to dislodge. Julius Nyerere appeared to recognize this point in 1960 when he offered to delay Tanganyika's own independence in the interest of establishing an East African federation with Kenya and Uganda, which were not yet themselves independent. Already the establishment of separate regimes in Transkei and the Ciskei has inhibited the cause of a political

7. See, for example, the *Financial Mail*, August 19, 1977, pp. 669–71.

union between these areas because of competition between their respective leadership.

Second, it is obvious that the entrenchment in office of multiple African prime ministers further increases the difficulty of coordinating their views and commitments. Thus the net pressure they mount on the Pretoria regime, is inevitably reduced—as the phrase "divide and rule" has it—lessening the chance for greater white concessions of land and resources.

Third, independence tends to legitimize and thereby permanently fix territorial boundaries, as confirmed by the failure thus far of Transkei's efforts since independence to engage Pretoria on the question of additional land. The time for boundary adjustments clearly is before independence (or perhaps after an ensuing clash).

The fourth reason has to do with the public image of official policy. To the extent that Transkei independence has been understood by Africans and others in South Africa as, in Turk's words, "a cover for continuation of white domination," it has stigmatized *any* separatist plan as fraudulent.[8] Pretoria's Bantustan program has given the separatist ideal, even in the abstract, a bad name, making the job of building support for true separatism more difficult than it might otherwise have been. Indeed, it is probably true that *any* plan emanating now from Pretoria that falls short of the twin principles of "one-man, one-vote" and "majority rule" will evoke great suspicion.

Finally, given the variety of interests that would inevitably have to be accommodated through processes of compromise and concession in any plan for real partition, there would seem to be practical advantage in dealing with all these interests at once in a single, grand settlement. To approach these issues piecemeal, each in isolation from the others, would seem much more difficult from the standpoint of the negotiations involved. A few of the writers considered deal directly with the question of the sequential "timing" of decisions leading to a separatist result. Evidently, however, all of them contemplated a pattern of change that would be both fairly rapid from start to finish and concurrently geographically compre-

8. Turk, "The Futures of South Africa," p. 410.

hensive. It is frankly difficult to imagine South Africa, in its present context, incrementally easing into a successful race partition of its territory.

Why does official policy fall so far short of what a partition solution would seem to require? One reason, to be treated in the next section, is that Pretoria has conceptualized "partition" differently from the way we have, but a second reason pertains to the perceptions most whites in South Africa have of their own position. Although nearly all whites recognize that their society is under great pressure, as a group they are hardly desperate. Some among the whites interpret the urban riots of 1976 and 1977 in South Africa as the opening round in a lengthy and expanding race war in the region, but there are many more who continue to dismiss this possibility. Clearly, as all the writers cited point out, true partition would necessarily require appreciable and lasting sacrifices on the part of the privileged whites. But as those privileges are thought by many whites to be secure for the immediate future under present policies, it is scarcely surprising that there are relatively few individuals ready to give up their privileges now in order to avert a distant danger that is perhaps not fully appreciated. In context, segregation, in Turk's sense, is probably all the political process presently permits in a system in which only the whites have the vote. The obvious danger from the standpoint of those who wish a peaceful change in South Africa is that when the perceptions of the whites finally do allow partition to be "practical politics," the Africans may no longer be interested in negotiating. Indeed, some observers believe that this point has already been reached. This question will be taken up again. For now the general proposition is that an equitable partition of a territory among contending parties seems unlikely when the balance of political power at the time is heavily in favor of one of those parties.

Decolonization
The contention of this section is that although government spokesmen occasionally use the word *partition* when describing official race policy toward the African population, what

they actually have in mind (that is, *their* orientation) is different from partition as the concept has been used here and can more adequately be summarized as decolonization. Indeed, the characterization of white South Africa as a colonial power vis-à-vis the country's African population is well established and familiar. As long ago as 1952 Leo Marquard wrote as follows in the conclusion of his book *The Peoples and Policies of South Africa:*

> Perhaps the strangest contradiction, and the one that explains a good deal of what is happening in South Africa, is that this union of four colonial possessions has become itself a colonial power, with all the problems that face those European states that hold dominion over non-European peoples.

For Marquard the recommended response to South African colonialism was not the creation of independent African states from the reserve areas but rather some form of a racially integrated society. "In South Africa," he wrote, "the problem of the rulers is not how to assist Africans to self-government, but how to train them to be full citizens in a country in which black and white live side by side."[9] But it was inevitable that some others would see the advancement of Africans to self-government in the reserves as precisely the correct response to South African domestic colonialism.

The National party government's current view was made clear during the speech of Minister M. C. Botha, previously cited, at the time of introducing the Status of the Transkei Bill in parliament in June 1976.

> We are not dealing here with a process of isolation of either a Black or a White nation, because in isolation we cannot live here as neighbors. In fact, the matter revolves around the consummation of the natural course of development of a Black nation on the pattern followed by nations all over the world, throughout the ages, in attaining self-realization and fulfillment by developing separately.

9. Leo Marquard, *Peoples and Policies of South Africa* (London: Oxford University Press, 1952), pp. 238, 241.

This occurred in Europe and other continents with large States and smaller ones, and this was right and natural; it was accepted by all. Until recently this still occurred on our own continent of Africa, in fact on our borders and also encircled by our South African territory and also in the form of comparatively small States. This was also right, also natural, and they were also quite rightly recognized and accepted. Why and in what respect is the same process then wrong when it is now to take place in so far as the Transkei is concerned?[10]

Many other similar expressions might be cited, covering many years. And certainly, for his part, Prime Minister Matanzima endorses a view of Transkei independence rooted in the perspective of decolonization. In his "Address to the Nation," only moments after midnight on October 26, 1976, Matanzima stated,

It has been alleged in certain quarters that our independence is an essential element of South Africa's policy of apartheid. If this implies that Transkei is in agreement with or actively supports the racial discrimination which has, let us face it, for centuries, typified the so-called "South African way of life," I must reject it with the contempt it deserves! If it is meant or understood, however, that our independence is an essential element of the Republic of South Africa's own decolonisation effort which, in turn, is part of the *overall* pattern of twentieth century African decolonisation, then I must agree wholeheartedly.[11]

The significance from Pretoria's side of defining as decolonization the unfolding of South African race policy toward Africans is that in justifying that policy at home and overseas Pretoria can plausibly argue that the test of the policy's sincerity and success ought to be its similarity to the record of various European efforts at decolonization elsewhere at earlier times. In particular it becomes critically important whether or not Transkei, to take the case at hand, was objec-

10. *House of Assembly Debates,* June 7, 1976, col. 8307.
11. Matanzima, *Address to the Nation,* p. 2.

tively as worthy a candidate for sovereignty as were, say, Lesotho, Malawi, Swaziland, or Burundi at the time of their independence. It is thus not surprising that, as Transkei independence neared, a variety of publications were issued by offices of the South African government, each purporting to show that Transkei could stand the test of comparison with other new states of the world, particularly in Africa. Thus we learn in the July 1976 *South African Panorama* (pp. 14,17), for example, that Transkei is larger than twenty-two members of the United Nations, has a higher literacy rate than thirty-one members, and has a larger income than twenty-seven. (Note that the last statistic is correct only if the earnings of the migrant workers from Transkei who are away in the republic are included.)

The allusion in Minister Botha's speech to the examples of Botswana, Lesotho, and Swaziland is revealing, for there can be little doubt that the essence of Pretoria's grand strategy is to reproduce its current relations with the BLS countries and their citizens in South Africa with each homeland as it becomes independent and to have each new relationship accepted everywhere as fully legitimate as, for example, Pretoria's dealings with Swaziland. Indeed, as early as September 1963, when Prime Minister Verwoerd, speaking in the Pretoria City Hall, publicly renounced South Africa's long-standing ambitions to annex the three so-called High Commission Territories, he pointedly observed that Britain's plans that these three areas should, if they wished, become independent states were in fact no different from South Africa's own program for the political evolution of the homelands. Verwoerd's interest, and the interest of his successor, in having this analogy accepted is obvious and involves primarily two elements. First, it would appear to excuse the poverty and undeveloped nature of the homelands, for certainly they are no different in this regard from Lesotho. Moreover, Britain and France, at least, are clearly many more times wealthy than the African nations *they* sired, and one hears few complaints about this. Second, the model would seem to justify, if not the blatant petty-apartheid discriminations against them, at least the legal exclusion of the citizens of

independent Bantustans resident in the republic from participation in the political life of South Africa. After all, BLS citizens in the republic have no vote in the election of representatives to parliament in Cape Town.

However, the analogy fails for two reasons, one political
and one demographic. In the first place, the current citizens
of Botswana, Lesotho, and Swaziland (excepting perhaps
some naturalized persons) were never South African nationals,
as Transkei citizens were. Because of this and because of their
determined resistance during half a century to the incorporation of their territories into South Africa, which was anticipated in the South Africa Act of 1909, the idea did not take
root among them (as it did among Africans and other victims
of discrimination within South Africa's borders) that they no
less than the whites had a rightful claim to a democratic share
of the wealth and promise of South Africa. Thus, the assumption of Pretoria's thinking that South African Africans would
be politically satisfied with no more of a state of their own
than had previously appeared to satisfy the populations of
the BLS countries, would likely seem incorrect. Put differently, in terms of prevailing ideology, Transkei independence
involved "opportunity costs" for Transkeians that were not
perceived to exist by the populations of the High Commission Territories as those areas approached independence in
the middle 1960s.

The second point was touched on much earlier. Whatever
the personal and communal gratifications of being politically
independent, they are in the case of the BLS countries presumed to extend only to their resident populations and a
relatively small percentage of migrant workers. But, as seen
earlier, Transkei independence is intended, in Pretoria's view,
to gratify equivalent Transkei populations and, in addition,
some one million other Xhosa who are permanently resident
outside the borders of Transkei in South Africa. Even if it is
accepted that the de facto population of Transkei and Transkeian migrant workers have obtained the same sense of relief
from white domination because of independence as is presumed to be the case with the citizenry of, for example,
Lesotho, there are no grounds for assuming any change in the

prior attitudes and aspirations of the so-called urban Xhosa, or at least change in the direction of lessened tensions and racial accommodation. Indeed, some observers have speculated that the sure result of stripping the urban Xhosa of their South African citizenship can only be to heighten their sense of political frustration and desperation, thus increasing political tensions instead of reducing them.

This absence of an exact parallel between Transkei independence and the previous independence of Botswana, Lesotho, and Swaziland shows up in an interesting way in a comparison of population figures for the several South African homelands. This point has been mentioned briefly earlier but will be amplified here. The so-called urban Xhosa consist, of course, of many individuals who were born in the "white areas" of South Africa of parents or grandparents who came from Transkei. They were South African nationals on the grounds of birth but appear to have lost their citizenship in the republic on October 26, 1976. Obviously, in the early 1960s there were tens of thousands of other Africans who had been born in South Africa of parents or grandparents who came from one of the High Commission Territories. They too were South African nationals by birth, but when the High Commission Territories became independent, their South African citizenship was unaffected. What became of these people, who might be termed the urban Tswana, Swazi, or Basotho? It appears that they have merely been administratively assigned by Pretoria to a homeland of like ethnic quality, for we find that these homelands have a much higher than average percentage of their populations living in the white-claimed areas of South Africa. Figures supplied originally by Muriel Horrell and later refined by Butler, Rotberg, and Adams show that in 1970, 53.5 percent of the total African population of the republic lived in the white areas.[12] However, the comparable statistics for the Tswana (Bophuthatswana), the Swazi, and the Basotho (QwaQwa) homelands were 64.5 percent, 77.5 percent, and 90.1 percent, re-

12. Muriel Horrell, *The African Homelands of South Africa* (Johannesburg: S. A. Institute of Race Relations, 1973), pp. 37–39; Butler, Rotberg, and Adams, *Black Homelands of South Africa*, p. 5.

spectively. (The figure for the two Xhosa homelands taken together was 43.9 percent of their combined populations living in the white areas, including migrant workers.)

Indeed, the blatant absurdity of the Swazi and QwaQwa homelands as prospective sovereign states (818 and 141 square miles in area, respectively) suggests that Pretoria may have another purpose in mind for them. It is speculation, but I imagine that Pretoria hopes to offer the Swazi homeland for annexation to Swaziland, and the QwaQwa homeland to Lesotho. The price South Africa would hope to extract for such annexations would doubtless be the willingness of these independent governments to accept responsibility for the full populations of these homelands, especially those persons in the white-claimed areas. Were this done, Pretoria would have established an exact parallel, demographically speaking, between the independence of Swaziland and Lesotho and the independence of the homelands; and it may be that a similar strategy is contemplated with respect to Botswana, although the independence of Bophuthatswana in December 1977 is certainly a complicating factor. It goes without saying that it is difficult to imagine any of the independent BLS governments being willing to pay such a price, however much they may covet the territories in question.

Observers of Transkei independence from the perspective of decolonization emphasize the many undoubted, objective similarities between Transkei and some other independent African states, although concurrently they typically ignore the anomalous position of the urban Xhosa. In part because of this anomaly, Transkei is at this writing an outcast state in world affairs, which fact obviously undermines the value of Transkei independence for its citizenry and the whites of the republic. Still, from the standpoint of the de facto population of Transkei, and especially the previously identified beneficiaries of Transkei independence, there are some immediate, practical advantages to belonging to even an outcast state of one's own, if one considers the alternatives. Clearly this is Matanzima's view (for whom it is doubtless most true). But the perspective of decolonization, when articulated by the white regime, also assumes an immediate, positive, and direct contribution from Transkei independence to the realization of more harmonious race relations within the republic, and this assumption I find to be without foundation. It may be too severe to liken Transkei independence to a placebo given to the white population of South Africa that causes them to feel more secure without in fact altering the dilemmas of their situation. Shortly I will suggest some possible indirect benefits of Transkei independence for race relations beyond its borders. Still, it is hard to see the relevance of decolonization or of Transkei independence to the problems of the region as a whole.

Power-Sharing

By *power-sharing* I refer to the political incorporation by white South Africa of currently excluded, oppressed populations by means and to degrees that are expected (by its proponents) to lower political tensions to manageable levels (by reasonably democratic government), while not seriously jeopardizing the material or cultural interests of the whites. The compound word, *power-sharing,* is chosen to highlight the *group orientation* that underlies this perspective—the sharing of power by sociologically distinct groups—and sets it off from the more familiar twin principles of "one-man, one-vote" and "majority rule," with which the concept is to a degree in direct ideological competition. "Power-sharing" thus covers separatist "solutions" to South Africa's difficulties other than partition, that is, federalism, as well as other variants that are infrequently described as "separatist," although some would appear to have much in common with this point of view.

An assumption of this discussion is that it is grossly unrealistic to expect the white electorate of South Africa under any foreseeable conditions to accept voluntarily a political structure based on the above twin principles, because most of its members are convinced that such acceptance would be tantamount to their permanent political subordination to an African majority whose interests, if not necessarily hostile to those of the whites, at least diverge from them materially and culturally. Attainment of democratic majority rule in the near future is thus synonymous with revolution, although the reverse may not be true. The perspective of power-sharing does not ignore the *possibility* of violent revolution occurring in South Africa. Indeed, it takes the idea that it *could* occur as an important impetus for change among whites, together with the imperatives toward nonracialism that some believe are contained in capitalist industrialization.[13] Proponents of this view doubt, however, that successful revolution is likely, assuming that none of the major powers of the world actively enters the situation against the republic.[14] Public predictions that revolution *is* likely or just around the corner are taken to be mainly politically inspired rhetoric on the part of persons who *want* to see a revolutionary outcome. The view thus holds that the power of white South Africa is probably sufficient to contain and direct social and political change in the republic in the years immediately ahead, although not sufficient to block change altogether.

This is not to say that persons looking at South Africa from this perspective are generally confident that evolutionary, incremental, and peaceful steps of the quality indicated will ultimately produce racial justice in that country, although this is not ruled out. It is merely asserted that this is the most promising road toward racial justice now. This has been called the field of "second best" solutions to South Africa's racial dilemmas. Clearly it is conservative. Its proponents believe that what it typically lacks in moral passion is compensated for by greater realism.

Under the general heading of power-sharing, two separate themes can be identified, although in practice these are commonly intertwined. Heribert Adam has referred to one of these as "liberal reformism."[15] Its essence is a massive improvement in the economic conditions and economic bargaining power of the black (and particularly the African) working classes, coupled with the deliberate *embourgeoisement* of

13. For example, Michael O'Dowd, "South Africa in the Light of the Stages of Economic Growth," in Adrian Leftwich, ed., *South Africa* (London: Allison and Busby, 1974), pp. 29–44.

14. Adam, "Three Perspectives," p. 10.

15. Ibid., p. 15.

substantial segments of these populations, all calculated to
give black workers a stake in the societal status quo. Key suggestions include: (1) ending of the practice of migratory
labor and the development of a stable labor force, (2) recognition of African trade unions, (3) ending of the practice of
"job reservation," by which Africans have been excluded
from most skilled and supervisory positions, and (4) acceptance of the principle of equal pay for equal work and the reduction of the wage gap separating white and black workers
generally. Other points that are less narrowly economic are:
(5) elimination of the pass laws and official encouragement
of settled family life among African workers in the cities,
(6) ending of separate Bantu Education curricula for African
schoolchildren, (7) extension to universities, churches,
schools, sporting clubs, and the like, of freedom of choice in
the matter of the racial composition of their memberships,
(8) repeal of antimiscegenation legislation, and (9) elimination of so-called petty apartheid regulations generally. The
goal of these changes is the dismantling of official apartheid
and the creation in its place of a nonracial, pragmatic, class-
structured social order linked with international capitalism.
Adam, whose·writings allow for the possible evolution of
such a society in South Africa through incremental steps
brought about by recurrent cycles of pressure (including at
times some violence) and bargaining, has in conversation with
me characterized it as openly "neo-colonial."[16]

What is obviously lacking in the foregoing is a formal political dimension to "liberal reformism." For some this is a question best deferred on the assumption, in Adam's words, that
"any reformist improvement of basic living conditions or
education can only increase the likelihood of more fundamental changes later, not to speak of the moral case for continuing reform."[17] This is the argument that once the organiz-
ing capabilities of the excluded groups are enhanced, together
with their strategic position (that is, power) in the industrial

16. The best-known example of this writing is Heribert Adam,
*Modernizing Racial Domination: The Dynamics of South African Poli-
tics* (Berkeley: University of California Press, 1971), esp. pp. 145–84.
17. Adam, "Three Perspectives," pp. 13–14.

structure, increased political rights will inevitably follow. But the white electorate demands a more clearcut lead. The new Progressive Federal party proposes a qualified franchise based on education (Standard VIII [grade 10] minimum) that would incorporate a gradually increasing number of the nonwhite middle classes without, at least for a decade (when programs for countrywide compulsory education to Standard VIII would begin to be felt), challenging white political hegemony. This proposal builds upon the ideas of the new Progressive Federal party's organizational predecessors and returns to the much older "Cape liberal tradition" of "equal rights for all civilized men."

Yet as the associated constitutional proposals of the PFP (the most liberal of the parliamentary parties) attest, white voters in the aggregate are thought unwilling to commit their futures unconditionally to potential black majorities, despite how gradual that process might be. Accordingly, a second theme to power-sharing has been the construction, if only on paper, of political structures that would ensure, concurrent with unprecedented black participation at the national level (that is, at the center), individual and group rights and areas of virtual ethnic autonomy. To an American especially, many of the suggestions are familiar: federalism, under a rigid constitution; an independent judiciary with the power of judicial review of the constitutionality of legislation; a bill of individual rights; and a national government of limited and expressly delegated powers. Clearly, the drift of such thinking, which now belatedly and hesitantly includes the ruling National party as well, is toward the invention for South Africa of some form of ethnic *consociationalism,* which, following Hans Daalder, I define as a political union of segmented groups such that none loses its identity or substantial control over its own affairs, and within which interelite cooperation occurs with the deliberate aim of counteracting "the centrifugal forces at the level of the masses."[18]

In passing, it should be pointed out that apart from the failure of Pretoria to propose as yet significant power-sharing

18. Hans Daalder, "The Consociational Democracy Theme," *World Politics* 26, no. 4 (July 1974): 607–08.

with the Africans of the country, the prospects for consociational invention in South Africa would seem burdened by the apparent absence of conditions which some writers, after considering European examples, have come to regard as prerequisite, or at least as highly desirable, for successful consociationalism to occur. Among the alleged prerequisites, Arend Lijphart has listed two which it is difficult to say obtain in contemporary South Africa. One is that all elites have *some commitment* to maintaining the consociational system. If given the choice, it seems clear that representative leaders of the African population would prefer a system of simple majority rule, with all the costs that might entail.

Lijphart's second point is that the elites of each group must be able to transcend their own subcultures in order to work cooperatively with other elites. In Kenneth McRae's words, "According to this approach, much will clearly depend on the ability, mutual good will, and allegiance of the elites; *the role of leadership is crucial* [emphasis added]."[19] Here the deficiency would seem to belong to the whites, for there is little in the record of government dealings with black leaders over recent decades, and especially with the black leaders outside the homelands, to indicate that the Nationalists have this ability. Indeed, the government appears to have carefully avoided any arrangements with black leaders in the cities that would suggest joint decision-making.

The ability of the ruling Nationalists to work with coloured and Indian leaders, at least, should be clearer shortly, when information will be available on the workings of the newly proposed, multiracial Council of Cabinets, which seems destined to become the most important deliberative body in the land. Although whites are certain to be eight of the fifteen members of this body (there being also four coloured and three Indians), I am told that it is Pretoria's expectation that the council will reach decisions by consensus rather than by formal vote.[20] If this proves impossible, it is said that the

19. Kenneth McRae, ed., *Consociational Democracy: Political Accommodation in Segmented Societies* (Toronto: McClelland and Stewart, 1974), p. 8.

20. *South Africa's New Constitutional Plan.* Backgrounder (no. 10 of 1977) issued by the South African Embassy, Washington, D.C., p. 3.

state president, who will be the council's chairman, will decide, with dissenting members having no option but to withdraw. The majority will presumably wish to keep such an outcome infrequent because of its likelihood of exacerbating, in Lijphart's words, "disintegrative tendencies in the system."[21]

Other conditions supporting consociationalism that have been suggested are (1) the existence of a common external threat, (2) a balance of power among the several subcultures, (3) a relatively limited total load on the political system as a whole, and (4) popular acceptance of government by "elite cartel," implying publics that are minimally politicized.[22] But the undoubted external threat to continued white domination in South Africa is regarded by most blacks as a factor contributing to their own liberation. And although the Africans' far great numbers are perhaps offset by the greater material power of the whites, the latter superiority seems destined to erode, while the numerical strength of the Africans steadily increases. On the third point it can be observed that were liberal reformism in South Africa to succeed in muting not only racial confrontation but also latent class conflict, it could only be on the basis of welfare-state measures that have worked elsewhere, involving a significant redistribution of the wealth; the load on government would necessarily be great. Regarding the population's readiness to submit to rule by elite cartel, evidence exists only for the Afrikaners. The docile acceptance in the middle of 1977 by the ruling National party's provincial congresses of the cabinet's sweeping plans for constitutional reform underlines the degree to which government accountability, even to its own supporters, has atrophied in the contemporary republic.

How, then, may one evaluate Transkei independence from the standpoint of power-sharing? On the positive side, it seems possible to see Transkei independence as an important step toward a federal "United States of Southern Africa." Aside from the issue of independence, the present Transkei state approximates fairly well a constituent element in many of the federal plans for South Africa that have been devised from time to time, two of which (those of Leo Marquard and

21. McRae, *Consociational Democracy*, p. 8.
22. Ibid., p. 9.

Chief Gatsha Buthelezi) have previously been discussed. Certainly it would seem to establish a presumption in the increasing debate among whites regarding the most appropriate type of power-sharing arrangements (cantons, ethnic parliaments, and the like) favoring institutions with a territorial base, for the Transkei experiment in Pretoria's view has worked well. And note that the financial dependence of Transkei on Pretoria is less important in a federal perspective, for it is generally expected that in a federation wealth is transferred from the richer to the poorer units. The Transkei experience has also suggested a simple but effective resolution of the continuing problem of consolidating the African homelands: acceptance of the fact that after consolidation has occurred a minority population of whites, coloureds, and Indians may remain within a consolidated territory and be subject there to its African government. On this basis consolidation becomes merely a matter of relatively cost-free boundary adjustments rather than of an expensive buying out of whole minority populations. The implication, of course, which resulted in Pretoria's long resistance to the idea of a multiracial population in Transkei, is that if whites can live freely in an African-controlled area (leaving aside the issue of the franchise), Africans ought to be permitted to live equally freely in the white-claimed areas. Clearly not many white South Africans have as yet accepted this implication, but the fact of Transkei independence would seem to represent a pressure on them in that direction.

More generally, it seems arguable that Transkei independence has promoted power-sharing by exposing whites in South Africa, and particularly members of the white elite, to the unfamiliar picture of independent African political power. It must be acknowledged that contemporary relations between Pretoria and Umtata more closely resemble the consociational ideal—in that they require bargaining from independent power bases—than do relations between Pretoria and any other black entity within the country.

Finally, there is the matter of race relations themselves. Immediately, independence has eliminated legal apartheid from the territory and freed at the grass roots two million Africans from the control of the South African police, in context a significant achievement for those individuals. And, of course, independence represents a devolution of political power from whites to blacks within the territory. My presumption, for which there is as yet no known evidence, is that the ending of apartheid in Transkei undermines at least petty apartheid throughout the region through the power of successful example. Transkei is not, of course, the only non-racial or African-controlled state in southern Africa, but it is the only society that was previously legally subject to apartheid. It thus represents an interesting case study, albeit in a rural and a tribal area, of what can happen when local apartheid is abandoned and African political and administrative power becomes a reality.

It may be argued, however, that even if the conclusions of the preceding paragraph are granted, Transkei *does* now purport to be an independent state, and its future reaffiliation with a post-apartheid republic is therefore highly problematical. It is thus contended by some that the path to power-sharing, which is being suggested, runs grave risks of producing not a federal "United States of Southern Africa" but instead a number of weak ministates with little political, economic, or administrative coordination among them. The danger of this possibility must be conceded. Indeed, earlier in this chapter I allowed that political vested interests in Transkei would likely impede a union of the territory with other homelands in the future, because of a selfishness on the part of officeholders that is not unknown elsewhere in independent Africa. Yet, in the case now being discussed, the union would not be between mutually impoverished states but rather with an industrially strong heartland whose leverage over the periphery is already considerable. The material benefits to Transkei of reunion thus might outweigh the technical loss of sovereignty. (The motivations of the leaders of the heartland are, of course, another matter and might themselves burden the process we are envisaging.) Indeed, on just the second day of Transkei independence, October 27, 1976, speaking to international journalists in Umtata, Prime Minister Matanzima willingly entertained the idea of Transkei's becoming part of a larger federation on the model presented by the individual American states (though Matanzima's knowledge of the U.S. system is unclear). And in his autobiography, issued at about the same time, he wrote:

> I have repeatedly expressed my belief in a Federation of States in this sub-continent of Africa. The independent Transkei would no doubt make a vital contribution to the political and economic interests of such a Federation.[23]

In such a way, then, Transkei independence might in time prove to be an important, if not direct, step to eventual power-sharing in the region through federation.

In three other respects, however, it is clearly a retrogressive step. First is the legal position of the urban Xhosa. One does not approach the social justice and political accommodationist goals of power-sharing by stripping persons of their citizenship in areas of their permanent residence. Such a step is obviously unrealistic and unfair, and removal of this anomalous situation would seem a precondition to any international recognition of Transkei.

The second point refers to the division of the wealth of South Africa that is implicit in Transkei independence. The notion of power-sharing assumes that all citizens will have some reasonable access to the benefits of the collective wealth of the society, but practically, in the case at hand, Africa's richest country has virtually disinherited two million of its poorest members. The voluntary annual contributions of Pretoria toward underwriting the Transkei budget, and the republic's support of the work of the Transkei Development Corporation are welcome short-term efforts of the whites to deal more fairly, materially speaking, with Transkei, but they do not altogether eliminate basic economic problems, and they are not necessarily permanent measures. Earlier, reference was made to the idea of a "Greater Xhosaland," incorporating Transkei and the Ciskei and all the land between, including the port cities of East London and Queenstown. In material terms this would more closely approximate the ideal I have in mind, although even this eventually would probably not remove the case for substantial annual subsidies from the region's economic core.

23. Matanzima, *Independence My Way*, p. 38.

The third point has to do with political pressure on the white regime. No one argues that power-sharing, as here defined, is presently the goal of the white government, certainly not as far as the urban African population is concerned, or that Pretoria could embrace power-sharing without extraordinary pressures being first applied. In this context, the unity of the homeland leaders and their individual refusals to accept independence for their homelands were regarded for a short time before March 12, 1974 (when Matanzima finally declared unconditionally for independence), as a source of particularly effective pressure on the regime. In breaking ranks, Matanzima thus appeared to set back the interests of Africans in South Africa generally.

A milestone in the drive for interhomeland unity was the first summit conference of the leaders of six homelands (Transkei, Bophuthatswana, Gazankulu, Ciskei, Lebowa, and KwaZulu), held in Umtata on November 8, 1973. At the end of this meeting the six leaders signed a statement containing eight resolutions, the second of which read as follows:

Having understood that:
(a) the idea of Federation is a long term policy [and]
(b) that Federation is vital to the Unity of the Black people, and bearing in mind that our people should be fully informed to the idea of Federation,
this Conference resolves that in principle the idea of Federation be propagated to the people by the various Homeland Leaders.[24]

In signing this document Matanzima thus appeared to pledge himself and Transkei to joint action. Chief Buthelezi commented on the Umtata summit and subsequent events in language whose very dignity conveys his deep disappointment and requires quoting at length.

We all thought that 1973 marked a watershed when leaders from all these areas called "Homelands" met at Umtata in September [*sic*] and repeated their commitment to the

24. "Resolutions of the Homeland Leaders in Conference at Umtata on the 8th November, 1973," typescript, p. 1.

1912 Bloemfontein ideal [that Africans pursue one common destiny]. These areas were acceptable at most as units of one multi-National Federal State of South Africa. At that time it seemed possible that "Homelands" could be used as bases for moving towards black unity than as bases for promoting black disunity. . . .

At Umtata, the leaders had stressed that black oppression had nothing to do with being Xhosa, Sotho, Tswana. . . . They decided in future to request, not separate meetings with the Prime Minister, but one conference where they would all deal with black problems, not on an ethnic basis. The first such meeting was held on the 6 March 1974.

It was however, not very long after this, when we read newspaper reports about joint meetings between the Prime Minister and the Chief Minister of the Transkei. . . .

I cannot say more than that the imminent "independence" of these areas [Transkei and Bophuthatswana] is cause for great agony in the hearts of many an African patriot. One must not give the impression that our brothers are not great patriots in their own rights. But if we look back at the Bloemfontein commitment in 1912 and the whole struggle I have referred to up to the Umtata Conference in September [*sic*] 1973, there is every reason for such agony.

One does not want to adopt a judgemental stance as to what this independence will mean, . . . But one can describe the pain of watching the glee in Nationalist circles, emanating from the feeling that they can now get away easily by saying that they are sincere about their policies, which to say the least are aimed at robbing black people of their birthright as South Africans. . . .[25]

In addition to the matter of Matanzima's having broken the ranks of the homeland leaders vis-à-vis Pretoria, Buthelezi's statement also raises the intriguing (and frankly, ultimately unanswerable) question of the "entitlement" of Transkei to withdraw from South Africa—or what might be

25. Chief Gatsha Mongosuthu Buthelezi, Untitled contribution to *Transkei Independence* (Durban: Black Community Programs, 1976), pp. 27–28.

termed the "historical mandate" for independence. Here I will digress briefly to consider this point. When Lesotho became independent in 1966, no voices are known to have been raised to claim that that step was improper or illegitimate, although much earlier in the century it has been widely assumed that the future of all three High Commission Territories lay in their eventual incorporation into the Union of South Africa. But by the 1960s much of the world appeared to welcome the step, indeed, perhaps to insist on it as a means of keeping the territory out of Pretoria's hands and free of apartheid. Yet, when a decade later Transkei claimed independence for ostensibly the same purpose, some individuals held that it had no right to do so.[26]

The implication would seem to be that in the history of southern Africa there arose, figuratively, at some point, a critical fork in the road. The inhabitants of Basutoland and the Bechuanaland Protectorate (as these territories were known before independence) and Swaziland chose, or at least went down one path toward, eventual national sovereignty, while Transkei went down the other path toward indissoluble union with the peoples, or at least the African peoples, of South Africa. But when, in the case of Transkei, did this critical choice occur, and who was entitled to make it on behalf of two million contemporary Transkeians? Certainly a key date is 1884, when Great Britain agreed to resume control of Basutoland, which had previously been governed from Cape Town. But Leonard Thompson notes that the "Scanlen ministry [of the Cape Colony] actually tried to persuade the British government to assume control over the Transkei as well as Basutoland; Britain, however, declined, and in 1885 the Cape Colony incorporated the remaining territories south of the Mthatha River."[27] The point underscores Matanzima's

26. See, for example, Oliver Tambo (acting-president, in exile, of the banned African National Congress of South Africa), "The Victory of Our Cause Is Assured." United Nations, Centre Against Apartheid, Department of Political and Security Council Affairs. Notes and Documents, no. 33/76, November 1976, p. 7.

27. Leonard Thompson, "Subjection of the African Chiefdoms, 1870–1898," in Monica Wilson and L. M. Thompson, eds., *The Oxford History of South Africa*, vol. 2 (Oxford: The Clarendon Press, 1971), p. 259.

charge that until recently Transkeians themselves were never consulted when critical decisions affecting their future were made—for example, the decision in 1910 to create the Union of South Africa, and the one in 1960 to transform it into a republic.[28] Buthelezi appears to suggest that the January 1912 Bloemfontein meeting of hundreds of African delegates, which established the South African Native National Congress (later the ANC) *was* such an occasion. It is not known who from Transkei attended this meeting, but it does seem probable that some Transkeians were present. Sheridan Johns, however, has noted that delegates attended from the "neighboring British territories" as well, a point that would seem to confound the conclusion that this meeting committed Transkei, but not Basutoland, permanently to South Africa.[29] Matanzima's signature to the November 8, 1973, "Resolutions of the Homeland Leaders in Conference," is less readily dismissed, although his authorization to make individually such a commitment to perpetual affiliation is unclear. This discussion highlights once again the seriousness of the omission of a popular referendum in Transkei on an issue as momentous for the territory as political succession.

Stalemate
There is one final perspective that requires mention, which is in fact a residual category in that it is predicated on the failure in practice of all the strategies previously mentioned to resolve the tensions of the South African conflict, including, particularly, the revolutionary and the power-sharing strategies that superficially seem the most promising. The failure of power-sharing appears the easier to foretell, for whatever the merits of suggestions for "democratic alternatives to the 'Westminster' model" that have originated over many years from a variety of individuals and groups,[30] it seems evident that the ruling Nationalists, notwithstanding their 1977 constitutional

28. Matanzima, *Independence My Way*, p. 28.
29. Sheridan Johns, ed., *Protest and Hope, 1882-1934.* Vol. 1 of *From Protest to Challenge: A Documentary History of African Politics in South Africa, 1882-1964,* Thomas Karis and Gwendolen M. Carter, eds. (Stanford: Hoover Institution Press, 1972), p. 61.
30. See, for example, Randall, *South Africa's Political Alternatives,* chap. 10.

proposals, are traveling too slowly along this path (if indeed it is conceded that they are traveling along it at all) to be able to cope with the subject peoples' insistent demands for change. Moreover, the inability of the Turnhalle proposals for South West Africa/Namibia to gain international acceptance, to say nothing of the various efforts of the Smith regime in Rhodesia to bring conservative blacks into that government, has conveyed throughout the region the impression that power-sharing formulae are always fraudulent. Austin's words are particularly apt here.

> "Power sharing", of whatever kind, would depend on its acceptance by the African majority, which may not like the idea at all: revenge is as powerful an emotion as self-interest, particularly when spurred by past injustice. Since a large part of the history of such internal transfer of power has been the record of too little too late, it hardly seems likely that South Africa would get it right.[31]

But does this not mean that revolution is inevitable? Certainly it means that pressures for revolutionary change—"seizing power" in the contemporary language of exile groups—will mount, including guerrilla incursions from neighboring territories and, in time, urban terror in the heartland. But there is some limited, if informed, opinion that holds, as indicated previously, that successful revolution is unlikely. Heribert Adam, for one, has written that "an unjust regime is not necessarily a faltering one," contrary to what many of the proponents of revolution in South Africa often appear naively to believe.[32] Yet it would seem that the efforts at revolution, though unsuccessful, would lessen all the more the chances for intergroup accommodation by increasing bitterness across the color line. In this perspective the South African conflict may be expected to tend gradually toward anarchy, in which the quality of life for everyone, white and black, would be destroyed.

Where would the process end? It seems possible that in a context of protracted political and, indeed, military stalemate, coupled with mutual fatigue and desperation among

31. Austin, "White Power: Cohesion Without Consensus?" p. 36.
32. Adam, "Three Perspectives," p. 1.

the parties, the idea of negotiated racial partition of the country could reemerge as a "last way out," a partition far more generous to African interests than any now contemplated, and one legitimized for Africans by the intensity of white sacrifice and the suffering that would have advanced the struggle to this point. (The occasionally heard suggestion of a de facto partition along borders that correspond to the battleline between confronting armies seems remote for two reasons. Almost any conceivable battleline would still leave millions of blacks behind white lines. And it seems unlikely that African military pressure on white South Africa would take the form of an army in the field occupying fixed positions and specific territory.)

In such an eventuality, would there be any relevance in the fact that Transkei is an independent state? The territory might be used as a safe haven for guerrilla groups, but this seems farfetched, given Umtata's economic and financial dependence on Pretoria. Moreover, unlike some of the other homelands, Transkei is relatively distant from the industrial centers of the republic and from concentrations of populations, which would presumably be the guerrillas' ultimate target. Nor is the leadership of Transkei likely to be effective beyond its borders, even in the limited task of providing "good offices" for the negotiations that would be required. In fact, it seems probable that the people of Transkei might be only spectators at such a procession of grim events, although of course one expects their sympathies would be with the African cause generally. I can foresee but one contribution of Transkei independence to this scenario, should it occur, and that a passive contribution: the vague presumption it gives in the thinking of many whites to partition as a "last solution" to the South African conflict. This presumption grows out of two observations. First, Pretoria's relations with the Transkei leaders in the context of Transkei separatism and with the homeland leaders generally are the most constructive relations Pretoria has with any Africans in the country. Under increased strain, it seems only reasonable that Pretoria would try to increase relationships of this type. And second, although various African nationalist groups in exile have spoken of the eventual reunification of Transkei with South Africa in a fully "liberated" subcontinent,[33] many observers accept Transkei independence as a permament and irreversible step. Thus, if other homelands do indeed follow Transkei's (and now Bophuthatswana's) lead, Transkei independence will have somewhat narrowed the range of options available to the country as a whole. It seems probable that in the future an increasing number of whites will be inclined to say, "We've already abandoned a substantial portion of the country to the Africans, so the power-sharing option for all of South Africa is no longer available; whether we like it or not we have become committed to partition as the only alternative to revolution or an endless civil war."

One final point must be made. In order for a political-military stalemate to occur in South Africa in the form discussed above, it would seem necessary for important centers of international power to remain neutral on the issues of the conflict, or if not neutral to be more or less evenly balanced. Otherwise it would seem that the party favored by the external world would assuredly triumph. But it is in this respect that the whites of South Africa may be different from the Israelis, who have American power committed to their interests, or from either side in the decade-old sectarian struggle in Ulster, neither of which has drawn appreciable international support. When, in the words of the title of a recent article on confrontation and accommodation in South Africa, "the chips are down," the trend of current events suggests that white South Africans might have to stand alone and thus be fully exposed against the opprobrium of much, if not most, of the rest of the world.[34] In the context of South Africa, then, the idea of a political-military stalemate may lack a critical prerequisite.

33. For example, see *Sechaba* 11, no. 2 (1977): 48.
34. Heribert Adam, "When the Chips Are Down: Confrontation and Accommodation in South Africa," *Contemporary Crises,* no. 1 (1977), pp. 417–35.

AFTERWORD

FINAL THOUGHTS
ON THE ISOLATION OF TRANSKEI

The underlying concern of this work has been conflict resolution, consistent with the title of the fellowship that supported the field research. I went to southern Africa in 1976
to see not only whether Transkei was as good a candidate for
sovereignty as, say, Lesotho, but also whether Transkei independence could increase racial justice in southern Africa as a
whole, would decrease racial justice, or perhaps was irrelevant
to the matter. I must emphasize that this has been a *regional*
concern, although most of the data have been drawn from
Transkei itself. This issue has now been considered from four
different, politically conservative perspectives, each of which
has also been regional in its focus. I discard the perspective of
decolonization on the grounds that it is inadequately matched
to the requirements of reducing tensions throughout the
region, but it is noticeable that the most optimistic interpre-
tation of Transkei independence, that of the power-sharing
perspective, has still been essentially, although not wholly,
negative. Transkei independence, I find, is largely irrelevant
to the political tensions of southern Africa primarily because
it does not honestly address these tensions where they are
most evident, among blacks in the cities. Indeed, Transkei

independence is detrimental to the cause of racial justice
in that it undermines the legitimate claims of urban blacks
for equal treatment where they live. It is thus scarcely surprising that after one year of legal sovereignty there is at this
writing virtually no support for Transkei independence
among the nations of the world, save for South Africa itself,
and now Bophuthatswana.

This international official ignoring of Transkei, epitomized
by the General Assembly resolution of October 26, 1976,
represents an unfairness to resident Transkeians who wish
their territory to be accorded recognition as an independent
state, for on all *conventional* measures there is no question
but that Transkei is as well qualified for independence as
some states that are now in the United Nations. Generally
these states are among the world's poorest and weakest, and
it would be wrong to believe that there are a great number of
them, at least in Africa, but clearly there are some. Yet all
governments are necessarily concerned (or at least profess to
be concerned) that any apparent acceptance on their part of
Transkei independence would seem to sanction and legitimate the stripping away of the rights of Africans in the cities
of South Africa. In his October 26, 1976, speech from which
we have quoted several times, Matanzima denied that under
Transkei law any such inference need be drawn from recognition, but most observers disagree with him on this point
and with his reading of the Transkei Constitution (despite his
essential authorship of that document). Certainly South African law makes clear that the urban Xhosa from Transkei are
no longer South African citizens and because of this have no
permanent rights in South Africa. Thus, when the U.S. House
of Representatives resolved (H. Res. 1509) on September 21,
1976, by 245 votes to 156, wi h 29 abstentions, that the
president should not extend diplomatic recognition to Transkei, the majority were clearly correct in stating that American recognition would be widely understood "as endorsement
of or acquiescence in the concept and practice of apartheid."[1]
The so-called citizenship issue is not the only problem with

1. U.S., Congress, House, *Congressional Record*, 94th Congr., 2d sess.,
September 21, 1976, H10636.

Transkei independence, but it is far and away the most important. At least in the West, therefore, the minimum condition for future recognition of Transkei would seem likely to be South African acceptance of the urban Xhosa as South African citizens, which theoretically would mean the end, or at least the fundamental recasting, of current South African race policy.

But were white South Africa in fact to abandon apartheid/ separate development, it seems probable that many, although not all, of those Transkeians who now favor independence might change their minds. The exceptional cases would be those individuals who have developed a personal stake in it: cabinet ministers, ambassadors, high-level civil servants, and the like. For most Transkeians in the territory, however, the principal value of independence is that it offers them the chance to escape apartheid. The irony of Transkei independence is that it is rejected by the nations of the world because they too oppose apartheid. The immediate effect of this rejection is to exile politically the inhabitants of the territory who are not themselves responsible for race discrimination and who eliminated it from their new state the first chance they had. Meanwhile, many of these same rejecting nations continue their previous association with Pretoria, whose policy *is* apartheid and which continues to insist on it within the republic's borders. In the bitter words of an African Transkeian official heard at independence, "South Africa has been charged by the world with race discrimination, judged and found guilty; but Transkei has been sent to serve the sentence."

If governments cannot reasonably be expected to recognize Transkei under current conditions, what about private individuals and organizations? Here there are two questions: what do private individuals think about Transkei and Transkei independence, and what activities are they prepared to sanction in, or with respect to, the territory. Obviously I am now addressing a different audience from that identified in the preface, namely, individuals outside the ruling circles of South Africa, and especially men and women of affairs outside the region altogether.

Attitudes. Because a governmental decision to recognize, or not to recognize, Transkei is necessarily a summary judgment, such a decision conveys the appearance of a *total* acceptance or *total* rejection of the state. It is thus a judgment that at least on the surface does not seem to distinguish between truly abhorrent features and those changes that might be welcome. From the radical point of view (if articles on Transkei appearing in the ANC periodical *Sechaba,* can be taken as an indication), Transkei independence *is* totally abhorrent, except perhaps as it provides a focus for discussions directed at delegitimizing the Pretoria regime. (On the other hand, as we have said, one hears rumors that some members of South African exile groups are privately considering whether Transkei independence does not offer more tactical possibilities than the public positions of these groups concede.) From the standpoint of power-sharing, however, there would seem to be some few features of Transkei independence that unquestionably represent an advance over what went on before, fundamentally the devolution to Africans of increased political control over their own lives, economic decentralization, and the ending of local apartheid. Governments perforce must face squarely the issue of official recognition. Private individuals and agencies are not so constrained. They have the right to an opinion more subtle and complex than a simple thumbs up or thumbs down outcome. And where such individuals and agencies believe that the future of South Africa will move, or ought to move, in the direction of greater power-sharing, it would seem they need not merely echo the radicals, but should have more discerning views concerning Transkei independence than simply that it does not adequately resolve the tensions of the region. The issues involved in Transkei independence are numerous and many of them are at best ambiguous. Thus, at least for the liberal, the quick dismissal of independence smacks of simplistic thinking.

This challenge to liberals (here meaning proponents of power-sharing) is not only on the matter of intellectual forthrightness, it also concerns the question of political adeptness. A problem (from the standpoint of conflict resolution) with many of the public pronouncements of opposition to apartheid is that in much general usage the term *apartheid* has come to signify *any* arrangement in South Africa that falls short of "one man, one vote" and "majority rule." But, as explained earlier, most white South Africans are bound to resist these principles. The debate thus tends to move away from, rather than to seek, a middle ground of acceptable compromise. Whites who might entertain the power-sharing proposals of Chief Buthelezi, cited earlier, or of the Progressive Federal party, are discouraged from doing so by the thought that should the day ever come when these or similar proposals can be implemented, there will be many who will continue to attack these ideas, charging that they constitute apartheid in a new guise. The point is that the *categorical* rejection of Transkei independence strikes many white persons of influence in South Africa as showing a closed-mindedness and, if not a commitment to their political destruction, at least an insensitivity to their plight. It thus reduces their receptivity to criticism of their government's policies to below what might have been expected had such criticism focused on specific shortcomings of Transkei independence while concurrently indicating the acceptability of other elements. Normatively speaking, there is no reason why the plight of the whites should receive more of our attention and sympathy than the plight of the blacks, including here the coloureds and the Asians. Indeed, given the history of black suffering in the region, the opposite is clearly called for. But for the moment the whites of South Africa, and particularly the 60 percent who are Afrikaners, have a near monopoly of legal power, which they show no signs of relinquishing. Thus if, as the proponents of power-sharing do, one contemplates incremental reform of the political structure rather than its overthrow, one logically would seem required to follow strategies that would increase rather than decrease the influence of outsiders with these holders of power, without of course losing sight of the purpose of that influence—reform directed toward power-sharing. Such influence can result from pressures, certainly (economic, diplomatic, and the like), but persuasion too is essential when dealing with a proud and stubborn people, which most observers have found the Afrikaners to be. This then is an argument for attacking Transkei independence not in general, but at its weakest point, or points. As Dennis Austin has observed, "if the community of nations can find a place for Djibouti, there ought to be room for Transkei."[2] It is just not credible in Pretoria that Transkei independence should be all wrong.

Activities. The issue of whether or not private individuals and institutions (for example, the International Red Cross) should endeavor to go to Transkei in order to pursue their special and varied interests within its borders is more complex, for clearly this cannot be done without first dealing with the Transkei government, and this constitutes a de facto recognition of the Transkei state on the part of these individuals and bodies. The danger, of course, is that such de facto recognition could in time be used somehow against the legitimate interests of Africans in the cities, although exactly how this might occur is not immediately clear. More difficult still is the issue of material assistance to Transkei, either in the form of direct investment or philanthropic aid. Should the level of foreign assistance to Transkei grow appreciably, the lesson for the other homelands in South Africa would be obvious; they too would be encouraged to seek legal independence, jeopardizing (or at least confusing) the claims of their "citizens" to a more equitable share of the riches of southern Africa and the improved "life chances" such greater wealth could support.

The response of some individuals and agencies to these implications, including the UN General Assembly, as seen earlier, is to urge the *total* isolation, or quarantine, of Transkei until more general political changes in the region are forthcoming. Thus, travelers to Transkei now run the risk of being labeled "accomplices of apartheid," and overseas

2. Austin, "White Power in South Africa: Cohesion without Consensus?" Typescript, no page. This statement was deleted from the published version of this article.

bodies such as the Nieman Fellowship Program at Harvard University may be wary of inviting Transkeians to participate, lest they too be drawn into the controversy. As a short-term tactic, quarantine of Transkei might be morally tolerable if it could be demonstrated that it was a necessary part of an overall strategy for change in the region that would stand a good chance of producing positive results within a relatively brief period. But as an *indefinite* posture toward 2.3 million territorial Transkeians, only a handful of whom could be remotely held responsible for the circumstances of their state, it is far more difficult to accept, especially when the individuals arguing for such a policy are not prepared (as clearly some are) to quarantine the republic as a whole. Unlike some others, I anticipate that the abandonment of apartheid, though certain, will be a slow and incremental process. From this perspective, then, while acknowledging that quarantine of Transkei (and now Bophuthatswana) would actively discourage other homeland governments from following in their path (as official nonrecognition of the two states already does), I find the idea objectionable for three interrelated reasons. First, even if all of the remaining homelands should refuse to choose independence, this would not significantly contribute to the downfall of apartheid. It seems more likely that the ultimate failure of current official race policy will result primarily from events and pressures arising both in the cities of South Africa and overseas. Second, while quarantine would not help end apartheid, it would represent outside intrusion and pressure on the freedom of the homeland populations themselves to cope with the fact of the apartheid state. And finally, of course, while quarantine would most likely have little positive effect, it would significantly harm the interests of the Transkei people. Except as a reservoir for cheap labor for the industries of white South Africa, the people of Transkei *have* been ignored throughout this century until very recently, with the result that, by contemporary world standards, nearly all of them are "have nots," materially speaking. If one is critical of past policy for failing to have included the people of Transkei in the overall development of the subcontinent, it seems one should not wish to perpetuate that isolation needlessly now.

Of course poverty is a characteristic common to all the African homelands in South Africa, and, indeed, this observation suggests a principle for private dealings with Transkei: namely, that activities that are acceptable, say, in KwaZulu and the other "African areas" of South Africa should be acceptable, from an international point of view, in Transkei as well. Or alternately, undertakings that were generally deemed proper in Transkei before October 25, 1976—mission work, health support, commercial investment, educational exchange—should be deemed proper thereafter, although some contact with the Transkei government is obviously necessary for this to occur. I respect private individuals and bodies who wish to avoid appearing to reward the people of Transkei for having taken legal independence, as would be the case if the level of private assistance to Transkei were to increase greatly without a corresponding increase among the African homelands in South Africa. It *is* responsible to wish not to encourage the populations of these other areas to jeopardize their participation in a future democratic South Africa. But I believe that these same individuals and bodies should be similarly respected if they do not wish to appear to punish Transkei for the same step. For, in context, the options that were available to territorial Transkeians in the middle 1970s to purge apartheid from their own lives were exceedingly limited. The fact of the matter is that in pressing independence on Transkei, Kaiser Matanzima, although he has lived most of his life away from whites and is in some respects a strikingly traditional and undemocratic figure, has delivered more in the way of *actual* African emancipation from white oppression in southern Africa than any other individual in history to date. Some insist that this achievement is still very circumscribed and compromises larger and more general gains in the future. This may or may not be true. Meanwhile, it is hard not to be sympathetic to the standpoint of Umtata, which is summarized by the proverb, "Better is halfe a lofe than no bread."[3] It is a bold individual who can say confidently that the alternative to their taking legal independence offered adult Transkeians resident in the territory more than, or even as much as, that step itself.

3. John Heywood, *Proverbes,* Part I, chap. 11.

Postscript

Just seventeen and one-half months after the final lowering
of the South African flag in Umtata, Transkei unexpectedly
broke off diplomatic relations with the republic. The date
was April 10, 1978, although the South African ambassador
to Transkei, Daan Potgieter, was given three weeks to close
his office and return home. This sudden rupture came well
after the end of the period covered by this study, of course.
But the irony of Transkei's breaking its only link with the
outside world and seeming to jeopardize continuation of
Pretoria's essential budget support commends some brief
mention here and an effort to gauge its possible significance.

According to remarks of Matanzima in the National Assembly at the time, the precipitating event was the transfer of the
area known as East Griqualand in the republic from the Cape
Province to Natal, a few days before. As previously seen, the
prime minister had long coveted this nearby land for Transkei.
"To us," he said, "it [the transfer of East Griqualand] is a
declaration of war against Transkei." Nonetheless, Transkei
would "bide its time before taking up arms to recover the
land that has been cynically raped from it."[4]

Speculation in the press focused on two other possible
explanations, however. One was the suggestion that Matanzima hoped his public break with Pretoria would create widespread sympathy for Transkei throughout the world and
open the way to international recognition and assistance.
Pledges by Matanzima that Transkei would now "join the
liberation movement and claim the whole of South Africa"
for the black-controlled majority seemed calculated to produce this result.[5] The other explanation concerned Transkei's
domestic politics. In the opening weeks of the 1978 session
of the Transkei National Assembly, sixteen TNIP members
defected to the opposition. The government's majority in the
150-member parliament was still an overwhelming 106 seats,
but as all but one of the defectors were from the important

4. *Africa Research Bulletin: Political Social and Cultural Series,* 15,
no. 4 (May 15, 1978): 4817.
5. Ibid.

Eastern Pondoland region (which had given Matanzima critical support in his 1963 victory over Victor Poto), observers
sensed these changes might portend a more sweeping realignment of political forces to come. In this perspective some saw
the break of diplomatic relations as a near-classic example of
a political leader's seeking to bolster sagging domestic prestige by fermenting an international crisis with an unpopular
foreign power.

A bizarre feature of the estrangement of the Western
Pondo from TNIP was Matanzima's abrupt sacking, in Novem-
ber 1977, of the only woman member of his cabinet, Stella
Sigcau, who is also the daughter of the Transkei president,
Paramount Chief Botha Sigcau of Western Pondoland. Matan-
zima later professed to have been offended by the fact that
Sigcau (a widow) had become pregnant, apparently as a result
of an affair with ambassador-at-large (and former minister)
Chief Jeremiah Moshesh. Ethnically a Basotho, Moshesh was
himself dismissed from the government the following March.

By June 1978 it was clear that the breaking of diplomatic
ties with Pretoria had not created a tide of sympathy for
Transkei in the world beyond South Africa. There was no
way of knowing if, behind the scenes, African liberation
groups might be attempting to take up Matanzima's offer of
assistance, although this seemed unlikely. But no state is
known to have responded to Transkei's undisguised eagerness
for recognition, while much of the world's press continued to
ridicule the idea. On the other hand, while South Africa's
position on the future of East Griqualand remained unchanged,
the republican government did not attempt to retaliate against
Transkei. In particular, Prime Minister Vorster indicated in
Cape Town that economic assistance to Transkei would continue as before, although military support and advisers were
withdrawn. South Africa appointed an agent to handle its
affairs in Transkei, which suggested that the two governments
would continue to deal with each other, albeit in a shadowy
fashion. Only in the realm of domestic politics did there
appear to be any benefit for Matanzima. The *Africa Research
Bulletin* reported that his defiance of South Africa made him

"a national hero" at home and reunited the assembly behind him on this issue.[6]

Yet despite this short-term value to the prime minister, the episode overall bespeaks the fundamental desperation of his position and that of Transkei, as well as the unpredictability of one-man rule. Having played what amounts to its trump card, Transkei is still isolated in the world, it is still materially dependent on South Africa, and East Griqualand still remains in the republic. Transkeians in the aggregate doubtless have derived some symbolic gratification from this thumbing of the nose at white South Africa and from the expression of solidarity with the rest of Africa that the gesture represents. But as the diplomatic break is increasingly perceived to have no effect on the reality of white power in the region, enhanced group pride could give way to group humiliation. The pressures on Matanzima for ever more extreme demonstrations of resentment against Pretoria must certainly mount, but the ability of the South African regime to discipline truly unwanted behavior on the republic's borders is formidable. The crux of Matanzima's foreign affairs problem is that Transkei needs more from others—jobs, financial assistance, recognition—than others need from Transkei. Thus while attacking white South Africa to build support within Transkei and/or curry favor with the United Nations is an obvious strategy for Matanzima, it is probably not a very promising one. It seems unlikely that by diplomatic means alone Transkei can escape from the awful material dependency and political isolation of its situation, especially while it is under the leadership of an individual who has previously appeared willing to accept both.

6. Ibid., 4818.

SELECTED BIBLIOGRAPHY

This listing updates to 1977 the bibliography of materials relating to Transkei that was included at the end of the Carter, Karis, and Stultz volume, *South Africa's Transkei* (1967). A recent bibliography of materials concerning the homelands generally will be found at the end of the book by Butler, Rotberg, and Adams, *The Black Homelands of South Africa* (1977). As they note there, extensive bibliographies for South Africa can be found in Heribert Adam, ed., *South Africa: Sociological Perspectives* (London: Oxford University Press, 1971), covering the period 1960-70, and in Leonard Thompson and Jeffrey Butler, eds., *Change in Contemporary South Africa* (Berkeley and Los Angeles: University of California Press, 1975), covering the period 1970-74.

Backer, W., ed. *The Economic Development of the Transkei.* Papers read during a symposium presented by the Fort Hare Economic Society, August 1969. Alice: Lovedale Press, 1970.

Barrie, G. N. "A legal view of Transkei recognition and so-called 'Statelessness'." *Politikon* 3, (October 1976): 31-35.

Bell, Trevor. "Bantustan Economic Development." *Third World* 2, (June 1973): 30-34.

Berger, Alan. "Mass Population Removals." *Third World* 2, (June 1973): 36-40.

Blaustein, Richard. *Britain and the Bantustans.* London: Bow Publications, 1974.

———. "Foreign Investment in the Black Homelands of South Africa." *African Affairs* 75 (April 1976): 208-23.

Blenck, Jurgen, and Klaus von der Ropp. "Republic of South Africa: Partition a Solution?" *Aussenpolitik* 27 (October 1976): 310-27.

Breytenbach, W. J. *Bantutuislande: Verkiesings en Politiek Partye.* Pretoria: Africa Institute, 1974.

———. "Chieftainship and Political Development in the Homelands." *Africa Institute Bulletin* 13 (1975): 328-33.

———. "The Political System of the Republic of Transkei—an Overview." *Politikon* 3 (October 1976): 36-51.

———. "Recent Elections and the Political Parties in the Homelands." *South African Journal of African Affairs* 4 (1974): 71-80.

———. "The Transkei Constitution in the African Context." *Africa Institute Bulletin* 14 (1976): 245-52.

———, "Transkei: Vague Guarantees." *To the Point.* (September 17, 1976), p. 21.

British Anti-Apartheid Movement. "The South African Bantustan program: its domestic and international implications." Memorandum to the United Nations Special Committee Against Apartheid, October 1975. United Nations, Unit on Apartheid, Department of Political and Security Council Affairs. Notes and Documents, no. 36/75, November 1975.

Bromberger, Norman. "Economic Growth and Political Change in South Africa," In *South Africa: Economic Growth and Political Change,* edited by Adrian Leftwich, London: Allison and Busby, 1974.

Brownlee, W. T. *Reminiscences of a Transkeian.* Pietermaritzburg: Shuter and Shooter, 1975.

Bundy, Colin. "The Emergence and Decline of a South African Peasantry." *African Affairs* 71 (October 1972): 369-88.

Bureau for Economic Research re Bantu Development (Benbo). *Black Development in South Africa.* Pretoria, 1976.

Butler, Jeffrey, Robert I. Rotberg, and John Adams. *The Black Homelands of South Africa: The Political and Economic Development of Bophuthatswana and KwaZulu.* Berkeley: University of California Press, 1977.

Campion, Harvey. *The New Transkei.* Sandton, South Africa: Valiant, 1976.

Carter, Gwendolen M. *Separate Development: The Challenge of the Transkei.* Johannesburg: S.A. Institute of Race Relations, 1966.

Carter, Gwendolen M., Thomas Karis, and Newell M. Stultz. *South Africa's Transkei: The Politics of Domestic Colonialism.* Evanston, Ill.: Northwestern University Press, 1967.

Cave, N. "The Transkei: Its Potential and Problems." *Barclays National Review* (September 1976), pp. 2-9.

Charton, Nancy C. J. "Black Elites in Transkei." *Politikon* 3 (October 1976): 61-74.

Copelyn, John Anthony. "The Mpondo Revolt, 1960." Unpublished B.A. (Honors) dissertation, University of the Witwatersrand, 1974.

Cramer, Philip A. "The Transkei and Third World Development." In *South Africa's Transkei,* edited by Glen Moss, pp. 12-18. Mimeographed. Johannesburg, 1976.

de Keyser, Ethel. "Bantustans: Myths and Realities." *Africa,* no. 43 (March 1975), pp. 31-33.

Diederichs, N. *Speech by the State President on the Occasion of the Independence of the Republic of Transkei.*

Folkscher, G. C. K. "The Economic and Fiscal Relationships of the Transkei vis-à-vis the Rest of the Republic as Determinants of its Economic Development." *South African Journal of Economics* 35 (September 1967): 203-18.

Grobler, J. H. "The Agricultural Potential of the Bantu Homelands." *Tydskrif vir Rasse Aangeleenthede* 23 (January 1972): 37-43.

Hahn, Lorna. "What Should the U. S. Do?" *Africa Report* 21 (May–June 1976): 6-10.

Hammond-Tooke, W. D. *Command or Consensus: The Development of Transkeian Local Government.* Cape Town: David Philip, 1975.

———. "The Transkeian Council System, 1895-1955: An Appraisal." *Journal of African History* 9 (1968): 455-77.

———. "Tribal Cohesion and the Incorporative Process in the Transkei, South Africa." In *From Tribe to Nation in Africa: Studies in Incorporation Processes,* edited by Ronald Cohen and John Middleton, pp. 217-41. Scranton, Pa.: Chandler Publishing Co., 1970.

Hart, Gillian Patricia. *Some Socio-Economic Aspects of African Entrepreneurship. With Particular Reference to the Transkei and Ciskei.* Grahamstown: Occasional Paper no. 16, Institute of Social and Economic Research, Rhodes University, 1972.

Holt, Basil. *Where Rainbirds Call. A Record of the Transkei.* Cape Town: Howard Timmins, 1972.

Horrell, Muriel. *The African Homelands of South Africa.* Johannesburg: S.A. Institute of Race Relations, 1973.

"Independence: A special survey of the Transkei." Supplement to *To the Point.* October 8, 1976.

Innes, Duncan, and Dan O'Meara. "Class Formation and Ideology: The Transkei Region." *Review of African Political Economy,* no. 7 (September–December 1976): 69-86.

Inter-Southern African Philatelic Agency. *Transkei.* Pretoria: Heer Publishing Co., 1976.

Ireland, Ralph R. "Transkei: The Significance of Education for the Development of the Republic of South Africa's First Bantustan." *Plural Societies* 3 (Spring 1972): 39-58.

Johnstone, Frederick A. "White Prosperity and White Supremacy in South Africa Today." *African Affairs* 69 (April 1970): 124-40.

Kirby, Alexander. "South African Bantustans: What 'Independence' for the Transkei?" United Nations, Centre Against Apartheid, Department of Political and Security Council Affairs. Notes and Documents, no. 26/76 (October 1976), pp. 1-9.

Kolbe, Kolya. "Power and Privilege in a Bantustan—The Transkei." In *South Africa's Transkei*, edited by Glen Moss, pp. 1-10. Mimeographed. Johannesburg, 1976.

Kotze, D. A. *African Politics in South Africa, 1964-1974: Parties and Issues*. Pretoria: van Schaik, 1975.

———. "Bantoe-owerhede in die Transkei: Werksaamhede en probleme." *Journal of Racial Affairs* 17 (July 1966): 19-28.

Kotze, H. J. "The Transkei General Election." *Africa Institute Bulletin* 6 (1973): 349-52.

Kotze, Hennie. "The Transkei General Election." *Africa Institute Bulletin* 14 (1976): 339-42.

Krause, Otto, P. J. Nieuwenhuizen, and C. J. van der Merwe. "The Implications of Transkei Independence." Transkei series no. 1. Braamfontein: S.A. Institute of International Affairs, 1976.

Laurence, Patrick. *The Transkei: South Africa's Politics of Partition*. Johannesburg. Ravan Press, 1976.

Leeuwenberg, Jeff. *Transkei: A Study in Economic Regression*. London: The Africa Bureau, 1977.

Legassick, Martin. "Legislation, Ideology and Economy in Post-1948 South Africa." *Journal of Southern African Studies* 1 (October 1974): 5-35.

———. "The Dynamics of Modernization in South Africa." *Journal of African History* 13 (1972): 145-50.

Legum, Colin. "Political Leadership in the Bantustans." *Third World* 2 (June 1973): 16-20.

———. "The Principal Leaders: Who's Who." *Third World* 2 (June 1973): 15-16.

Leistner, G. M. E. "Transkei: External Economic Relations." *Africa Institute Bulletin* 14 (1976): 263-65.

Lipton, Merle. "Independent Bantustans?" *International Affairs* 48 (January 1972): 1-19.

———. "The South African Census and the Bantustan Policy." *World Today* 28 (June 1972): 257-71.

Lombard, J. A., and P. J. van der Merwe. "Central Problems of the Economic Development of Bantu Homelands." *Finance and Trade Review* 10 (June 1972): 1-46.

Maasdorp, Gavin. *Economic Development Strategy in the African Homelands: The Role of Agriculture and Industry*. Johannesburg: S.A. Institute of Race Relations, 1974.

Madavo, Callisto E. "Government Policy and Economic Dualism in South Africa." *Canadian Journal of African Studies* 5 (1971): 19-32.

Malan, Theo. "Transkei—Economically Viable?" *Africa Institute Bulletin* 14 (1976): 253-62.

Malan, Theo, and P. S. Hattingh (compilers). *Swart Tuislande in Suid-Afrika*. Pretoria: The Africa Institute, 1975.

Malinga, Phineas. "Transkeian Cats Out of the Bag." *The African Communist,* no. 69 (1977): 35-41.

Marais, R. M. "In Re Transkei Independence." Typescript. Legal opinion rendered in Cape Town, June 3, 1976.

Maree, Johann. "Bantustan Economics." *Third World* 2 (June 1973): 26-29.

Maree, Johann, and P. J. de Vos. *Underemployment, Poverty and Migrant Labour in the Transkei and Ciskei.* Johannesburg: S.A. Institute of Race Relations, 1975.

Matanzima, Kaiser D. *Address to the Nation on the Occasion of the Declaration of Independence, 26 October 1976.*

―――. *Independence My Way.* Pretoria: Foreign Affairs Association, 1976.

Matatu, Godwin. "South Africa: The Transkei Fraud." *Africa,* no. 62 (October 1976): 11-16.

Mayer, Philip. "The Tribal Elite and the Transkeian Elections of 1963." In *The New Elites of Tropical Africa,* edited by P. C. Lloyd, pp. 286-311. London: Oxford University Press, 1966.

―――. *Urban Africans and the Bantustans.* 1972 Hoernle Memorial Lecture. Johannesburg: S.A. Institute of Race Relations, 1972.

Mitchell, Colin, and Fiona Wilson. "The Transkei: What It's Like Living With Blacks." *Personality,* May 3, 1974, pp. 38-43.

Mühlemann, Christoph. "Transkei—A Special Case." *Swiss Review of World Affairs* 27 (September 1977): 22-24.

Naude, C. F. Beyers. "The Balkanization of South Africa." *Africa Report* 21 (May-June 1976): 16-17.

Ndamse, C. M. C. "Address at the University of Witwatersrand." Mimeographed. September 1969.

Niewenhuysen, John. "Economic Development in the African Reserves of South Africa." *Land Economics* 42 (May 1966): 195-202.

Norman, Geoffrey E. "The Transkei: South Africa's Illegitimate Child." *New England Law Review* 12 (Winter 1977): 585-646.

Olivier, W. H. "Aspects of Transkei Citizenship and Nationality." *Politikon* 3 (October 1976): 75-84.

―――. "Soewereiniteit vir die Xhosa van die Transkei." *Journal of Racial Affairs* 26 (October 1975): 152-62.

Pollock, Norman. "The Transkei: An Economic Backwater?" *African Affairs* 68 (July 1966): 250-56.

Prinsloo, D. C., ed. *Transkei: Birth of a State.* Conference Report no. 2. Pretoria: Foreign Affairs Association, 1976.

Raynor, William. "Bantustans and Migrant Labour." *Third World* 2 (June 1973): 34-36.

Republic of South Africa. Department of Information. "Focus on Transkei," *Bantu* 22 (November 1976).

―――. Department of Information. *Multi-National Development in South Africa: The Reality.* Pretoria, 1974.

————. Explanatory Memorandum on the Status of the Transkei Bill, White Paper 12, 1976.

————. *Panorama* 21 (July 1976).

————. Transkei Government. *Debates of the Transkei Legislative Assembly.* Umtata: Elata Commercial Printers. Published annually, 1964-1976.

Republic of Transkei. *Annual Report of the Public Service Commission, 1976.*

————. *Debates of the National Assembly.* Second Session, First Assembly (9 March 1977 to 3 June 1977). Umtata: Elata Commercial Printers, 1977.

Rogers, Barbara. *Divide and Rule: South Africa's Bantustans.* London: International Defence and Aid Fund, 1976.

————. *South Africa: The "Bantu Homelands."* London: International Defence and Aid Fund, 1972.

Roos, Herman Willem. "Die Ontwikkeling van die Transkeise Regeringsdiens." Unpublished M.Admin. thesis, University of Pretoria, 1975. Typescript.

Rubin, Leslie. "Bantustan Policy: A Fantasy and a Fraud." United Nations, Unit on Apartheid, Department of Political and Security Council Affairs. Notes and Documents, no. 12/71, March 1971.

Rubin, Neville. "Constitutions of the Bantustans." *Third World* 2 (June 1973): 12-14.

Rutman, Gilbert L. "The Transkei: An Experiment in Economic Separation." *South African Journal of Economics* 36, (March 1968): 24-31.

Schlemmer, Lawrence. "City or Rural 'Homeland': A Study of Patterns of Identification Among Africans in South Africa's Divided Society." *Social Forces,* 51 (December 1972): 154-64.

————. "White Attitudes to the Bantustans." *Third World* 2 (June 1973): 41-44.

Schrire, Robert. "The Emancipation of Transkei." *The World Today* 33 (January 1977): 34-38.

Sibeko, David. "The Sham of Independence." *Africa Report* 21 (May-June 1976): 14-17, 56.

Sigcau, Paramount Chief Botha, president of Transkei. *Address to the Nation on Independence Day, October 26, 1976.*

Slabbert, F. van Zyl. "Modernization and Apartheid." In *Anatomy of Apartheid,* edited by Peter Randall, pp. 61-88. Johannesburg: Christian Institute of Southern Africa, 1970.

Socikwa, A. L. M., ed. *Inkululeko: The Independence of Transkei, A Political Backgrounder.* London: South African Embassy, 1976.

Southall, Roger J. "The Beneficiaries of Transkeian 'Independence'." *Journal of Modern African Studies* 15 (1977): 1-23.

————. "Independence for the Transkei: Mystification and Diversion in the Model Bantustan." Typescript.

Strauss, J. "Ontstaan van die Xhosa-regerings in die Transkei en die Ciskei en Verwagte Sosiopolitieke Ontwikkelings in die Gebiede."

Journal of Racial Affairs 22 (January 1971): 11-21.

———. "Selfstandigwording van die Transkei—Geboorte van 'n Selfregerende Staat." *Journal of Racial Affairs* 17 (October 1966): 20-31.

Stultz, Newell M. "Economic Viability of Transkei—An American View." *Africa Institute Bulletin* 15 (1977): 169-73.

———. "Transkei Independence in Separatist Perspective." *South Africa International* 8 (July 1977): 10-26.

———. "What's Wrong with Transkei Independence?" *Plural Societies* 8 (Spring 1977): 17-34.

Szeftel, Morris. "The Transkei: Conflict Externalization and Black Exclusivism." In *Collected Seminar Papers on the Societies of Southern Africa in the 19th and 20th Centuries,* Institute of Commonwealth Studies, Vol. 3 (October 1971-June 1972), pp. 155-73. London: University of London.

Tambo, Oliver. "The Victory of Our Cause is Assured." Statement made in plenary meeting of the General Assembly on October 26, 1976 by the acting president, African National Congress of South Africa. United Nations, Centre Against Apartheid, Department of Political and Security Council Affairs. Notes and Documents, no. 33/76, November 1976. Also printed in *Sechaba* 11 (1977): 6-17.

"The Transkei: An Account and Analysis of Bantustan Policy." *Sechaba* 11 (1977): 38-48.

Transkei Development Corporation. *Information for Potential Investors in the Transkei.* Mimeographed. April 1976.

Transkei: Economic Review, 1975. Pretoria: Bureau for Economic Research re Bantu Development, 1975.

Transkei Independence. Durban: Black Community Programs, 1976.

Transkei In Dependence. Report of the Transkei Study Project. Mimeographed. Johannesburg: Wages and Economics Commission, SRC, University of the Witwatersrand, 1976.

"Transkei: The Myth of Independence." *Sechaba* 10 (1976): 1-5.

Transkeian Government. *Republic of Transkei Constitution Bill.* Special Gazette, no. 1, April 23, 1976.

———. *Standing Rules of Procedure of the Transkeian Legislative Assembly, and Transkei Constitution Act, 1963. (Act no. 48 of 1963), As amended.* Durban: Drakensbergpers, n.d.

"Transkei's Initiation into Nationhood." *Financial Mail (Special Report),* October 22, 1976.

Trapido, Stanley. "South Africa in a Comparative Study of Industrialization." *The Journal of Development Studies* 7 (April 1971): 309-20.

van der Merwe, Hendrik W. "Changing Attitudes of Whites Toward African Development." Reprint no. 12. Rondebosch: The Abe Bailey Institute of Interracial Studies, University of Cape Town, pp. 106-20.

van der Merwe, P. J. "Central problems of economic development of Transkei." *Politikon* 3 (October 1976): 36-51.

Vigne, Randolph. *The Transkei—A South African Tragedy.* London: The Africa Bureau, 1970.

————. "What Are the Bantustans?" *Third World* 2 (June 1973): 5-11.

Villiers, J. "Bantustan Myths and Realities." *The African Communist,* no. 64 (1976), pp. 83-92.

Vorster, M. J. "The Transkei Constitution: Manifestation of diffusion and rediffusion of constitutional technology or Westminster transplanted?" *Politikon* 3 (October 1976): 85-105.

Wilson, Francis. *Migrant Labour.* Johannesburg: The South African Council of Churches and SPRO-CAS, 1972.

Woods, Donald. "Transkei independence: South Africa's calculated risk." *Optima* 25 (1975): 199-223.

Wronsley, R. P. "The Evolution of Public Administration in the Transkei." *Saipa: Journal for Public Administration* 7 (March 1972): 4-36."

Xhosa Development Corporation. *Ten Years of Progress: XDC in the Xhosa Homelands.* Tenth Annual Report, 1975.

Yudelman, David. "Industrialization, Race Relations and Change in South Africa: An Ideological and Academic Debate." *African Affairs* 74 (January 1975): 82-96.

INDEX

179